BEYOND

THE COLORFUL
COAT

To Anna Mae
Blessings await you!
Jeremiah 11:29

Lydia

BEYOND

THE COLORFUL COAT

Living Out Your God-given Dreams

Lydia Chorpening

ISBN: 978-0-9832016-5-6

Published and printed in the United States of America by:

LIFE SENTENCE Publishing, LLC
404 N 5th Street
Abbotsford, WI 54405
www.lifesentencepublishing.com

'Like' this book on facebook!

Available from the Publishers at:
(at the price of your choice)
www.lifesentencepublishing.com
715.223.3013

Also available from:
www.amazon.com

Available as ebook

Dedication

*I*t is with great joy that I lovingly dedicate this book to my husband of forty-two years. Russell has been patient with me as I have struggled with myself and fumbled in the publication process of my first book which is now in this exciting new and updated format. Russell has been my shoulder to cry on and the voice of encouragement when I needed it. Thank you, Russell for your dedicated support and for always being there for me even when you were suffering.

Table of Contents

Foreword

When I was introduced to the manuscripts and was asked to read Lydia Chorpening's literary *'Beyond the Colorful Coat'*, I was at first hesitant to read another book about the life of Joseph.

Other noted authors had already penned their own biographical writing about the ancient patriarch whose life story occupies more space in the book of Genesis than any other single individual.

But what a pleasant surprise and pleasure it was for me to read this beautiful allegory of *'Beyond the Colorful Coat'* which is symbolic to the freedoms that Christ brings into our lives as we continue our walk with Him. The book is about freedom from emotional and spiritual bondages that often go unaddressed in people's lives because of lack of understanding.

Lydia is gifted by God and qualified to address these spiritual issues. Her insight into each robe that Joseph wore from his place in the pit to his position in the palace will help the reader discover how God's plan for Joseph's life reveals his purpose for our lives.

I commend Lydia for hearing from God and penning her insights into the writing of this wonderful book.

I recommend *'Beyond the Colorful Coat'* for your reading and promise that you will receive new insights into God's grace that will add stature to your spiritual life and strength to your walk with God.

Virgil Amundson
Shell Lake, WI
Lydia's Pastor and friend

Introduction

$\mathcal{B}$EYOND THE COLORFUL COAT is actually an updated version of *The Seven Robes of Joseph,* a book that I had previously authored. God is giving me the opportunity to move beyond my mistakes made during the publication process of *The Seven Robes of Joseph.* I now have the privilege to update, reshape and to rededicate the message given to me through the inspiration of God.

This new edition reaches beyond the former messages. With today's end-time urgencies upon us, we must know how to deal with our own soulish issues to embrace Matthew 24: 6 *"...ye shall hear of wars and rumours of wars: see that ye be not troubled: for all these things must come to pass, but the end is not yet."* (KJV)

This means that we must push beyond the rumors, the fear and the anxiety of this age. Although I know that part of what Christ prophesied in Matthew chapter 24 concerning the destruction of the temple has already come to pass, we are seeing the fulfillment of Matthew chapter 24 in our generation. We are not to expect calamities, poverty and wars to cease. We also cannot anticipate less persecution for true Christians of today. Do you know how to live free of fear? Do you know how to go beyond these obstacles?

There are people who have gone before us who have left us a pattern of their overcoming lifestyle. These have pressed beyond the adverse circumstances of life to obtain their God-given inheritance.

Though this book is devoted to the life of Joseph, I am also giving special honor to a beautiful lady that moved beyond the perils, poverty and persecutions of her life. This influential person was small in stature, excelled with only a third grade education, abounded on meager means and still lived her years with dignity, concern for others and unquenched love.

She identified with Paul's words in II Corinthians 4:7-10; *"But we have this treasure in earthen vessels, that the excellency of the power may be of God, and not of us.*

We are troubled on every side, yet not distressed; we are perplexed, but not in despair;

Persecuted, but not forsaken; cast down, but not destroyed;

Always bearing about in the body the dying of the Lord Jesus, that the life also of Jesus might be made manifest in our body." (KJV)

My mother was born in 1912 and was the oldest of eight children. She gave birth to 7 living children, one of whom died at the tender age of two and a half. Mother worked hard all her life. She rose above hardships by singing praises to God while tears rolled down her gentle face. She lived a life of forgiveness as she pressed beyond the barriers which would have kept most people enslaved to blame, bitterness and unforgiveness.

She never gained much recognition during her lifetime, but she left us a pattern of how to move beyond the unfortunate, the unfamiliar and the unwarranted. She wasn't rich or famous, but she exhibited the raw material of faith, the substance that a Christian's life is made of.

Although I cannot give you a full review of my mother's last week on earth, I will give you a glimpse of it. She was living in a nursing home which she called her "little apartment". She had taken her neighbor, who had dementia, into her care. Mother saw to it that Lavina got to her meals on time and brought her to church and other activities. At the age of 98 ½ she had not forgotten how to love, to give and to bless.

Five days before she went home to be with Christ, she was rushed by ambulance to the emergency room. Though the caring staff tried their best to replenish the blood she was losing, their efforts proved futile. Even though she seemed to rally when she saw us arriving from our various states, we realized it was her time to leave us and go to her eternal home. She insisted on being out of bed on Saturday and was sure she was not sick. My sister-in-law, Marlene, played the piano in the hospice unit while our mother sang hymn after hymn with us that afternoon.

Until she was no longer able, she grasped everyone's hand, the doctors, nurses and visitors, then she pulled their hands to her lips and kissed them, saying "God bless you"

She was very aware that the next day was Easter Sunday. She refused to go to sleep on Saturday night and continued exhorting us. She sang her love songs to her Savior throughout the night. The last song we heard her sing was a line of an old German hymn that the Amish had sung: "Hot Zien laben fer mich gaben". My sister timed her and she sang this over and over for more than five minutes. The literal translation of this is, "Has His life for me given!" We knew Who she was looking at in her almost comatose state.

At one point during the night she pushed back her sheets, raised her hands heavenward and toward the foot of her bed. She lifted her head off her pillow and then her shoulders. She remained in that position for an extended length of time. Even though I have no way of knowing how long she stayed in this position, I know that this was a supernatural experience. She had been so weak that it took several nurses just to move her in and out of her bed. I was personally blessed to witness this 'beyond the visible' experience.

She breathed her last breath on earth on April 25, 2011. All of her children and our spouses were around her as she was leaving. We sang songs of celebration and spontaneously recited her favorite Scriptures as she moved beyond this earth to abide with the One she loves more than any other.

This little lady had touched the lives of many who lived in her small community. They flooded the funeral parlor during her viewing and her funeral service was nothing less than the ultimate celebration of her life. We were endowed with a legacy that no money can ever buy. Our beautiful mother imprinted our hearts with her lifestyle. She showed us how to endure to the end and how to triumphantly soar beyond this life on earth!

I dedicate the upgraded publication of this book, not only to my husband, but also to my late mother, Catherine (Katie) J. Borntreger.

With the publication of this redefined version on the life of Joseph, I also dedicate myself afresh and anew to be more Christ-like, more obedient to the Holy Spirit's leading and more tenacious in spreading the Good News of Jesus Christ.

I pray that your faith will mature as you follow Joseph's guiding example.

Preface

Part 1

I saw Joseph released from his ancient prison in which he had been bound by Egyptian history and the consequences of his soul. Through a miracle of faith I saw him unshackled from the chains of time, location and demotion. I heard the noisy, clangorous clatter of Joseph's fetters as they fell to the dungeon floor and echoed into this post-modern society.

I was compelled to walk with Joseph as he extended his hand to me across the span of time. I saw that his imprisonment started with what we will call, "soul-junk." I watched carefully as he forged beyond the bondages of his own heart and reached true liberty and freedom.

I heard the footsteps of conquest as he approached the Pharaoh for his promotion from prison to the palace. I've also discovered that Joseph's God-given faith proclaims his message which speaks beyond his casket and his grave.

In this guide, Joseph and I invite you to walk with us as he points out the landmarks of the Old Testament. His testimony resounds as he marches rank to rank with other descendants of

Abraham. Watch as he extends his heart of compassion to Job in his afflictions.

Because the Word of God has always been present, it allowed Joseph to take refuge in the book of Psalms. He now assures us of the same promises he drew his assurance from. We will be refreshed as we linger at chapter 23. *"The Lord is my shepherd"*...this is He who gave His life for us! *"I shall not want"*...I shall have provision, promotion and praise. *"For thou art with me"*...You know my where-about and won't forsake me. *"Surely goodness and mercy shall follow me all the days of my life and I shall dwell in the house of the Lord forever"*...I shall live beyond this life on earth!

From the book of Proverbs we identify many of Joseph's characteristics of wisdom, integrity, honesty, godliness, righteousness, sexual purity, trustworthiness, dependability, humility and responsibility.

With awe we embrace the prophets' anticipation of the Messiah's coming. This narrative enables us to break the bonds of time and circumstances and march beyond the Old Testament and into the New.

Look! Here is a parallel! Jesus extends His hand along with Joseph's. They both exemplify the process of discipleship. This parallel leads us through the miracles of Christ, his death, burial, resurrection and beyond to our own victory.

As Joseph leaves the entrance of the Christ's empty tomb he again bids us follow him through the precepts of the epistles and right into the book of Revelation. Here we affirm our own overcoming lifestyle as we note his diligence in keeping himself unspotted and undefiled by the world.

Joseph's example, our faith in 'God's Word' and this guide will walk us through the process of refinement into the transforming revelation of Jesus Christ. The Holy Spirit will lead us from the pages of inspired history into God's glorious and victorious church in the world today. As Joseph's life closely represents the life of Christ, he will lead us to the redemption of our God-given dream.

Preface

Part II

Because of the redemptive work of Christ in my own life, I would like to have you see where Christ has brought me from. So before we step into Joseph's boyhood, let me show you a glimpse of my own dysfunctional childhood. Before I begin, please remember as you read this that my story is my own. It is also my aim to help you understand that even a young child can overcome the pain and suffering of it's childhood with faith. However, because I was untaught, I did not know Christ in a personal way. I was in bondage to religion without having an intimate relationship with a loving and caring God.

Because of God's healing in my own life, you will understand the mandate I've been given to speak this message of moving beyond our confining "soul-junk" and into completion and wholeness in our Lord Jesus Christ.

Here's an early part of my story:

I was a very excited five year old, with shivers chasing each other up and down my spine. It was seldom that I had the privilege of leaving home except for our twice-a-month church attendance. Today church would be held at my uncle's place…my favorite!

My dad had just brushed his long dark beard that hung down onto his chest as he reached for his black, felt hat with its two-week's accumulation of dust. He looked very handsome in his dark blue three-piece suit. The starchy smell of his white shirt had replaced the odors that defined him as a hardworking man.

My mother scurried about in her bare feet trying to get everyone ready for the big event.

Lydia as a child

"Gricht mich myh shoe, Liddie (Get me my shoes, Lydia)," my mother hurriedly called in my direction. I scampered off to retrieve her high-top black shoes from under her sagging, unmade bed in the front room. After tying my little sister's black satin head covering, she placed her little black bonnet over that.

In preparation for the occasion, my mother had stayed up late, heating flat-irons on our wood range in the kitchen to iron our long black or dark blue dresses. She helped my brothers get dressed in their best homemade 'surge' pants and suspenders.

"Put on your straw hats," she called after them as they headed out the door, following their dad to the barn.

As my mother finished braiding my long dark brown hair, which fell well below my waist, she braided in a piece of string at the end and wrapped the braid up on the back of my head. After she had securely tied my black satin head covering under my chin, I put on the black bonnet that was traditional attire for a buggy ride to church.

Just as my mother started getting herself ready, the newest member of our family, born on Christmas day, started fussing for her diaper change and feeding. The four month old had patiently waited her turn for attention. Now Mother turned to her just before we all headed toward the front yard where the horse and buggy were waiting under our big hickory tree.

Dad's strong arms lifted me into the back of the open buggy, seating me between my brothers on the rough buggy bed. My sisters were tucked in with my parents on the spring-wagon type seat as we started down one of Missouri's rutted country roads.

The warming spring sun had already risen above the eastern horizon as Pat, our workhorse, made short distance of the mile that we had to travel. This new season had started to spread a blanket of fresh green grasses along the ditch as our red clay fields awaited cultivation and planting. Pat's familiar odor of horse sweat drifted to the back end of the buggy as we turned up the lane to my uncle's house.

You may think of the Amish lifestyle as being charming, but my story could hardly fit into such a setting. My emotions immediately swung from excitement to nervousness as I saw the various buggies that had preceded us. I felt paralyzed by shyness as Dad dropped us womenfolk off at the house. As we made our way inside I clung to my mother's long black skirt in fear of losing her in this crowd of women that were hugging and greeting each other.

How strange it was to see all the beds I used to hide under, and tables I used to sit at, removed from their usual places. Now the furniture had been removed and the rooms were filled with wooden backless benches. I followed my mother into one of the bedrooms as the men filed quietly into the living room for the morning service.

The benches felt like concrete and I was sure my back was going to break right away. Was it better to sit up straight or slump? Neither brought relief to my impatience. The long, drawn-out, monotone German hymns were sung without accompaniment or parts of harmony. I knelt on the hard wooden boards with everyone else for the routine reading of the High German prayer.

After being seated again I restlessly swung my legs back and forth in an effort to chase away my boredom. A light pinch on my leg brought me to my senses.

What if I had to sit with my dad in the men's designated area? I had been taught at this early age that the men might think something bad about me (in my mind that could have been anything) if I sat with them. That fear was enough to keep me from asking questions or having a desire to find out what would happen.

Again I straightened my posture as my mother fanned herself with her hanky in an effort to stay awake. I felt itchy and uncomfortable as perspiration trickled down my back.

It was time for the preacher to begin his usual sing-song, drawn-out sermon when I was wonderfully surprised! A visiting minister from Kansas was introduced and started his message taken from Revelation 3:15, 16. As he spoke he had my full attention. He actually preached from his heart rather than from previously assigned texts as did the other preachers.

I was enthralled! I'd never seen anyone use hand gestures as he turned in the doorway, from one room to the other. He spoke to the men, the women, and the teenaged girls who lingered in the kitchen. The smirking on the back porch turned to silence as he addressed the young boys who had congregated there.

Using the High German Bible, he read, "I desire that you are either cold or hot, but because you're lukewarm I'll spit you out of my mouth." (Paraphrase mine) I wasn't quite six, but the words bypassed my young mind and touched the core of my being.

The point was emphatically made that we must not be lukewarm. I understood that it would be best to be hot, like the red coals in our pot-bellied stove. I realized that cool fresh water pumped from our cistern was more desirable than the lukewarm in the late afternoon water pail.

My mentality of defeat had already declared that I could never be red–hot for God, so I decided to be cold rather than lukewarm. Lukewarm people would be spit out of God's mouth…I cringed at the thought. My decision left me sad and empty. A war was going on inside of me although I had no idea what I was dealing with.

Later in the afternoon I was silent as Dad flicked the reins onto Pat's back heading us toward home. My parents busily exchanged bits of news they had gained from conversations over the usual after-church lunch of sandwiches, home-canned pickles and coffee.

I didn't know how to express what I felt from the morning's message, as communication skills were not areas of strength in our home. Rather than trying to voice my feelings, I stuffed them with my growing collection of negative feelings I had even as a six year old.

As the years passed, I became enslaved to the unpleasant circumstances that surrounded me. My struggles continued to weave fear, frustration and a failure mentality into an unrelenting net of negative emotions.

That fall I was six years old and walking two miles north to our parochial school with my big brother. I enjoyed being with girls of my own age that first year. During our recesses, four or five of us would link our arms over each other's shoulders and march about the schoolyard feeling as if we were queens of the premises. It was only natural for us all to jabber away in our usual Pennsylvania Dutch dialect.

However, as I entered my second grade in the one-room schoolhouse things were becoming more troubling at home. My dad owned an old-fashioned sawmill and spent long hours felling trees with his crosscut saw. To make his work easier he bought a two-man, gasoline-powered McCullough chainsaw. The weeks that followed brought arguments and hard feelings into our home as the church leaders confronted my dad's perceived worldliness.

These harsh words leaked through the cracks of closed doors and found their way into my tender heart, crushing me as they led to our being excommunicated by that denomination.

My whole world as I had known it was turned upside down. I was taken out of school and forbidden contact with my friends. Since I was too young to be a church member, I was caught in a tradition that forbade discussion of church issues among non-church members. I knew something terrible had happened, but wasn't told why I couldn't play with my cousins or why I wasn't welcome at my uncle's house.

What if our family was on its way to hell as I had heard through the cracks of the closed doors? What if I was part of my dad's unpardonable sin? The 'what if' questions replayed over and over in my mind, but without resolve.

Having missed half a year of school, it was decided I would be enrolled in second grade again instead of entering third grade. My older brother and I were now joined by our younger brother who made us a strange trio in the unfamiliar setting of the local one-room public school.

I never allowed the adventure of the change to kick in, instead withdrawing and hoping that nobody would see me or talk to me. Students were cruel, and the language barrier was a major issue. I didn't know much of the English language and wasn't allowed to practice it at home. Because we held on to the old traditions of strict dress, I was the only Amish-clad girl in my class. I loved the lavish pinks and reds the rest of the girls wore, but felt guilty for desiring such worldliness.

I found reading extremely difficult, communication impossible and spelling frustrating. I couldn't write my assignments correctly and humiliation further hindered my dreams of being an A student.

I was never tested for dyslexia, but instead I fumbled all the way through my formal education - up through eighth grade - without being diagnosed (a reality I stumbled onto later in life). By the time I reached my adolescent years I had internalized so many negatives that I spent weeks being physically sick.

Does it surprise you that I could not understand God's love, purpose, and plan for me? Well, I had no foundation of truth and faith. I didn't have a personal relationship with a loving God. As the years have passed I've learned there's release and complete freedom from the vices of the unregenerated soul as I now walk with Christ Jesus as my Savior and Lord!

The journey from that point, to where I now know of God's love and purpose, has been one of many tests. The circumstances around me, the trials I've been through, and the problems that I now face have no bearing on who I am in the Lord Jesus Christ. Though I am still being refined day by day I can declare that the transformed life God has given me is the reason for my excitement in sharing this message on the life of Joseph. No matter what your life has been up to this point, you can have his keys to victory and move beyond your past.

The Robe of Righteousness

~ Romans 4:19-22 ~

*I*t looks like it's time for introductions," graceful Rachel, with her dark features, said as we step back in time and into her world. Rachel's eyes dance in her youthful face, and her raven hair is barely visible from beneath her highly decorated *kaffiyeh* (head-dress).[1]

"Look Joseph, we have visitors from a time that is yet to be," she says.

Turning to us she continues, "This is my son, Joseph. He will soon be five years old."

The little lad's eyes sparkle with life as he bows to us. Rachel hands Joseph his sandals made of rough leather and palm bark soles and explains where we are.

"I'll tell you who I am and where you are since I can tell that you're new to this place and time. I am the favored wife of the Patriarch Abraham's grandson, Jacob. Jacob tends the sheep of my father Laban, and we live in Padan-aran, the place Jacob fled to over twenty-five years ago. Abraham spent his first years here before God called him to move to Canaan over 175 years ago," Rachel explains.

The gracious woman who is making us aware of our surroundings reaches for her young son's hand. "Joseph and I are on our way to the pasture where Jacob is grazing the sheep. I would love to have you join us as we head to the fields," she invites us.

At her invitation, I reach for your hand and invite you to take this journey back into time to release Joseph's story from its ancient history. His life will soon liberate our own lives as we keep stride with Rachel's lively son and watch him grow and mature.

"We will have to hurry," Rachel speaks softly to Joseph as if she has forgotten us and focuses her full attention on the journey ahead of them.

JOSEPH LEARNS ABOUT FAITH AND RIGHTEOUSNESS AS A CHILD

Enthusiasm flashes in Joseph's face, bright as the late afternoon sunshine. Soon he is outside, hand in hand, with his mother. They make their way past the tents of his mother's handmaid Bilah, his Aunt Leah, and Leah's handmaid Zilpah. His older half-brothers, Reuben, Simeon, Levi and Judah, chase each other about the compound and pay no heed as Joseph and Rachel pass.

It isn't long until Joseph carelessly slips off his sandals and runs ahead of his mother. Rachel's step is graceful and determined, yet the little lad leads the way over the gently rolling hills. Joseph is full of life and loves the soft grasses that tickle his bare feet. His small sleeveless robe allows the sun to kiss his arms with warmth and strength.

Rachel catches up to Joseph as he scurries up a rock in hopes of seeing his father.

"Mother, why are we going to meet Papa tonight?" Joseph questions.

"It is a beautiful evening for a walk and if we get to the pastures early maybe your papa will have time to tell you a story," Rachel replies.

"I love Papa's stories. I can't wait to get there! See, Mama! Papa and his sheep are right over there. May I please run to him so he can start on his story?"

"I will run with you, Joseph!" Rachel answers.

Rachel hikes her long brightly colored skirt to her knees, and the two race across the distance as the horizon spreads an endless canvas of vivid pinks and lavenders high in the sky. Joseph seems tireless as he breathes deeply of the cool, fresh air in the open fields. The sight of his father energizes his steps. As the two near the shepherd, it is easy to see he is also wearing his simlah, a sleeveless, loose-fitting robe. Joseph giggles at the sight, knowing that his father will toss him high into the air with those strong arms.

"What brings you to the fields this refreshing fall evening?" Jacob asks.

Rachel blushes, "Why, it is you, of course, my dear. The day has been long, and we have come to talk for a bit."

Joseph is unable to contain his excitement any longer and interrupts, "Oh, Papa, Papa, we have come so you'll tell me a story! Mama said we might have time for one."

"What story would you like to hear?" Jacob asks, also being glad for someone to talk to.

"Tell me the story about my grandfather," is Joseph's ready response.

"I should have guessed the story you'd choose," teases Jacob with delight as he tossed Joseph heavenward and caught him again.

Knowing he is in for an eventful story, Joseph giggles as he settled onto a grassy spot left by the sheep.

"Come sit by me, my dear," Jacob motions to Rachel as he starts his story.

"There are three important facts that you must remember as I tell you this story. The first is that my grandfather heard God speak, the second is that he obeyed the command of God, and the last is that God honored my grandfather's faith and credited it to him for his righteousness. Do you know what righteousness is?"

Joseph is quiet for a moment as if in deep thought. "Didn't you say that righteousness was like a robe that we put on by faith over our heart?" Joseph asks.

"Yes, son, when you put on your simlah, your shepherd's robe, you use your hands to put it on. In the same way faith is a symbol of your hands and takes hold of righteousness to cover your heart," Jacob explains. "Because we believe our outward clothes carry great significance to our identification and feelings, so it is important for our hearts to always have on the robe of God's righteousness," Jacob continues. "Just as ministers, educators, and wealthy men wear only the meil-type clothes of a high ranking professional, so we, as God's children must never display anything from our heart except for God's righteousness."[2]

From there the story unfolds as the three sit with the sheep quietly grazing on the gentle slopes of Haran. "Abraham recognized God's voice as he commanded him to sacrifice his son, Isaac, and chose obedience to the command. My grandfather believed that God would raise his son from the dead if He actually required my father's life," Jacob says.

Joseph shivers as the sunlight wanes and at the thought of what could have happened. Jacob wraps Joseph into the folds of his own simlah robe to keep the young boy secure.

"God told Abraham to take wood, fire and his promised son to a mountain in Moriah that He'd point out to him. Obediently Abraham took Isaac, his thirteen-year-old son, up the mountain. On the way Isaac asked him concerning the sacrifice, 'You have wood and you have fire, but what about a sacrifice?'"

"Giving Isaac an answer of faith Abraham replied, 'God will provide the sacrifice that is needed,'" Jacob recounts.

Jacob explains that Abraham took rocks that he found on the mountaintop and built an altar. Then he tied his son and laid him on the altar.

Joseph quivers within the folds of his father's robe at the thought of his grandfather lying on the altar with his great-grandfather lifting the knife to slay him.

"It's alright, Joseph," Jacob reassures his young son. "Just in time God said, "Stop! Now I know you'll move beyond your fear and doubt to obey me. I see that you have not withheld your son from me. Now look in the thicket behind you and you'll find a sacrifice acceptable to me.'"

"Try to imagine how relieved your grandfather was when Abraham saw a ram caught by his horns in the thicket!" Jacob says.

Joseph sits in wide-eyed amazement realizing the goodness of God and how He had rewarded his great-grandfather's faith and obedience.

"Now remember, Son," Jacob breaks into his young son's deep thoughts, "my grandfather's faith was accredited to him for righteousness. Our faith in God becomes our righteousness in His sight. It wraps us in with God, just like I am wrapping you in my shepherd's robe. Your great-grandfather's faith was the spiritual robe he always wore. His symbolic robe is referred to as the 'robe of righteousness'. We can obtain our own robe of righteousness by faith and obedience."

By now daylight is fading, and Jacob calls his sheep as the three of them lead the sheep into the folds of Laban.

AN EVENING IN JOSEPH'S TEEN YEARS

By the time Joseph has reached his mid-teens, many changes have taken place in his family's life. They had left his birthplace and moved back to Hebron, the place of Jacob's ancestors. On their move back to Hebron Rachel had given birth to Benjamin, his only full-blooded brother. Sadly, Rachel had died during childbirth and left the two motherless. And Joseph now had ten half-brothers by his aunt Leah and the two handmaids.

Come, I hear Joseph calling us to listen in on a conversation he is having with his father. The early evening campfire is inviting as Joseph explains to us, "My father has told me many stories of faith and righteousness, but he has also shown traits of hanging onto past hurts. I would like for you to listen in on our conversation."

We sit where Joseph points to a grassy spot and listen as Jacob begins the conversation.

"I do so miss your mother, Joseph. When I first saw Rachel as a young girl, it was love at first sight. I served your grandfather for fourteen years until she was finally mine. But now she is gone."

Joseph pokes a stick into the fire thoughtfully. "Yes, Father, it is hard to be without my mother, but I do so love my little brother," Joseph tries to diffuse his father's downheartedness.

"Yes, son, we all love him; however, it is difficult for me to move past my loss and keep my mind fastened on that blessing. Many years ago when my father blessed me, before he sent me to Padanaram, these trials and woes of my life were never in my sphere of comprehension."

Joseph shifts his gaze from the flames of the open fire to the canopy of billions of stars that stud the skies with their jewel-like splendor. A soft breeze stirs the leaves in the olive tree nearby. "Papa," he reverts to his affectionate childhood name for Jacob, "from my earliest memories I recall you telling me of my great-grandfather's faith. I remember the account of your 90-year-old grandmother, Sarah, giving birth to your father. Papa, you told me of his obedience in offering his son on the altar and because of his obedience God spared my grandfather. You've explained how faith became Abraham's righteousness. You've told us that all it takes is faith to believe God's promises and when we exercise faith God credits it to us for our righteousness."

Jacob stirs restlessly as Joseph continues. "Do you remember the night long ago when we were still back with Grandpa Laban? You told me the story of Abraham's faith, and wrapped me in the folds of your robe, explaining how that shepherd's coat is like the robe of righteousness. Since then I've determined to live my life by faith and obedience to God. I attribute my trust and assurance to your teachings on nights like that when you held me close."

Jacob raises his shoulders and lifts his sight to the evening splendor at which his young son is gazing. "Marvelous, vast, fathomless," he whispers under his breath. Then he asks pointedly, "Joseph, do you sense that assurance of faith even when the times are hard?"

"Father, how could I but believe in the Almighty God when I consider the heavens, the work of His fingers, the moon and all these stars which He foresaw and created?" (See Psalm 8:3)

Jacob is thoughtful as he scans the flock of sheep that have settled nearby. "The sheep seem settled down so let's get some sleep before they begin to graze again."

Joseph rehearses the favor of God on his great-grandfather as he falls asleep, *"And not being weak in faith, he did not consider his own body, already dead (since he was about a hundred years old), and the deadness of Sarah's womb. He did not waver at the promise of God through unbelief, but was strengthened in faith, giving glory to God, and being fully convinced that what He had promised He was also able to perform. And therefore 'it was accounted to him for righteousness.'"* (Romans 4:19-22)

By the time Joseph has reached the age of seventeen he had not only learned to be a good sheepherder, but he also knew about the faith of his forefathers, although that faith still remained untested in him.

JOSEPH LIVED BEFORE THE LAW WAS GIVEN

Since Joseph lived before the Mosaic law and before the life and teaching of Jesus, we may ask, "How did Joseph acquire his robe of righteousness?"

Faith has always been the element that bridges the gap between man's humanity and the favor of God. The apostle Paul makes this clear in Romans 4:13-16 where he says, *"For the promise that he would be the heir of the world was not to Abraham or to his seed through the law, but through the righteousness of faith. For if those who are of the law are heirs, faith is made void and the promise made of no effect...Therefore it is of faith that it might be according to grace."* (Emphasis mine)

As the prophets looked forward in faith to God's redemption through Jesus, (Isaiah 9:6, 7) God chose to fulfill a destiny that reaches through the ages to us. Though Joseph lived before Christ's earthly birth, his faith was not void because Jesus was before all things (Colossians 1:17). This means that Christ was already present in Joseph's days.

Jesus said in John 8:58, *"Most assuredly, I say to you, before Abraham was, I AM."*

Another confirmation we have that Jesus is from the beginning is found in John 1:1: *"In the beginning was the Word, and the Word was with God, and the Word was God."* This verse spells out clearly that "the Word" refers to Jesus Christ.

The verification of Joseph's faith is clearly seen in 'God's Hall of Fame' in Hebrews 11:21, 22.

By faith Jacob, when he was dying, blessed each of the sons of Joseph, and worshiped, leaning on the top of his staff. By faith Joseph, when he was dying, made mention of the departure of the children of Israel, and gave instructions concerning his bones.

Joseph's faith, his appropriation of the robe of righteousness, and the fact that he was highly knowledgeable of his royal linage, cannot be questioned. Joseph's faith, though untested as of yet, marked his appropriation of God's righteousness.

Ephesians 2:8, 9 underlines the importance of faith for us.

"For by grace you have been saved through faith, and that not of yourselves; it is the gift of God, not of works, lest anyone should boast."

Faith is our necessary link to obtain God's righteousness in our own lives.

THE 'ROBE OF RIGHTEOUSNESS' - JESUS CHRIST IS THE DOOR INTO THE KINGDOM

Jesus is the only door, the only way, and the only opening for us to enter into the kingdom of God! We must personally understand the interest Jesus has in each of us. In John 10 Jesus declares Himself to be the door to the sheepfold. He fully realized his own flesh would be pierced in order for Him to become that door for us to pass through. Listen carefully to the heartbeat of Jesus in John 10:7-11.

"Then Jesus said to them again, 'Most assuredly, I say to you, I am the door of the sheepfold. All who ever came before Me are thieves and robbers, but the sheep did not hear them. I am the door. If anyone enters by Me,

he will be saved, and will go in and out and find pasture. The thief does not come except to steal, and to kill, and to destroy. I have come that they may have life, and that they may have it more abundantly.'"

In today's society it's not popular to narrow our choices to one and say that Jesus is the only way, and yet He declared the same in John 14:6 when He made proclamation to his disciples, *"I am the way, the truth, and the life. No one comes to the Father except through Me."*

Recently I attended an appreciation luncheon that ended in a form of meditation that focused on self rather than on Jesus. The speaker started his dialogue, "Be comfortable. Get into a position to relax and let yourself go. You may want to walk along some beach, or fly with the birds. Just let yourself be free."

Then I became aware of the wooing sound that arose from his brass meditation bowl. It filled the outer crevices of the room until it encircled the whole assembly. It ascended from an intriguing whisper to an alluring demand that summoned any resources coming within its grip. The instructor continued to urge us to relax by instructing us, "Always follow the light."

I was taken off guard by the turn of events at the lovely luncheon. With my daily access into the Spirit world through faith in Christ's finished work on Calvary, I knew that to have wandered out into this spiritual realm without entering through Christ would have classified me as a thief or robber. (See John 10:1) With only the loosely given guidelines there had been no mention of Jesus, the only spiritually legal authority granting us permission to enter into a supernatural realm.

That night my sleep was greatly disturbed; I felt I'd witnessed treason as those without spiritual authority had entered into a spiritual realm. I turned to God, and my prayerful surveillance brought me into clear focus.

In the beginning Satan was with God in Heaven. Heaven and earth were both God's territory until sin entered and Satan was cast out of Heaven. Thus Satan became the prince of the powers of the air and roams about as a roaring lion seeking to find someone to devour. (I Peter 5:8) The Bible describes him as a betrayer (John 13:2), as transformed into an angel of light (II Corinthians 11:14), a wolf that scatters (John 10:12), the serpent that beguiles (Genesis 3:4), and the father of lies (John 8:44).

After their arrest, Peter and John declared to the Sanhedrin that Jesus is the only door into God's spiritual kingdom. This strict sect of the Pharisees questioned the apostles about their spiritual authority, and they boldly declared the Name of Jesus, saying, *"Nor is there salvation in any other, for there is no other name under heaven given among men by which we must be saved."* (Acts 4:12)

Christ's bloodstained cross is our only legitimate door into the spirit realm. The wrongly acquired keys given in the earlier meditation session would give access to a cop-out mentality and aimless wandering. It holds humanity in a helpless vice while the assurance of Christ's death on Calvary, and His resurrection from the dead, provides a door of entrance for all humanity into the spiritual kingdom.

Jesus, our legal port of entrance into the spiritual realm, provides us with truth, purpose, integrity, guidelines, and structure for our meditations. He gives us legal access to appropriate, through faith, any promise in the Bible. He is the robe of Righteousness we must put on in order to serve and receive God as was intended in the beginning.

JESUS SPEAKS OF ROBES IN HIS PARABLES

In Matthew 22:1-12 Jesus compares the kingdom of heaven to a king who prepared a wedding feast for his son.

The king decked his house in splendid hangings of tapestry and prepared the finest foods, killing his fattened cattle and oxen for his invited guests. He sent his servants out with elaborate invitations to this elegant wedding. Those invited promptly ignored the royal summons due to their own desires and plans. With a heart for conquest, the king sent his servants out a second time with invitations and the urgent command, "Fill my house with guests." This time those invited mocked at the affair or treated the servants spitefully, even killing some.

This turn of events added anger to the king's determination. He quickly gave orders to his armies to destroy the murderers and annihilate their cities.

While his fattened cattle were still roasting in the ovens, he summoned his servants for the third time. "Go into the highways and alleys and bring in as many people as you can find." He gave a blanket invitation to each man, woman and child alike, without regard to their rank, color, or state.

As the guests arrived, the king, being a person of high rank, showed his lordly splendor and honored his guests by providing them a garment suitable for the festivity. Each was given a garment appropriate for the occasion.

There was, however, a guest who refused to wear the robe presented to him. When the king came to greet his guests, he was upset at seeing the defiance in this man. The robe had been freely given but so severely rejected. The king's majestic expression of generosity to the wayfaring man had been refused.

The king was furious and his command eminent! *"...Bind him hand and foot, take him away, and cast him into outer darkness; there will be weeping and gnashing of teeth."* (Matthew 22:13)

The robe the king furnished to his guests is symbolic of God's robe of righteousness generously provided for us. As the king's wrath is clearly seen when his invitation was scorned and the guest refused the suitable wedding garment, in like manner we'll incur God's wrath if we reject the righteousness He has provided for us in Jesus Christ.

Our Father's love and the importance of the robe of righteousness is clearly seen in Luke 15:11-32. Jesus tells the parable of a well-to-do farmer who had two sons. One day the younger of the two came in from the fields and demanded of his father, "Give me my inheritance".

The father tried to convince him of his poor choice, explaining the potential growth of his assets, but the son demanded the inheritance immediately.

With reluctance the father complied, and as he had suspected, the son soon left home and wasted all his possessions on prodigal living. Picture the son's plight when he found himself feeding a farmer's hogs during a severe famine and wishing to share some of the hogs' corn husks.

He had moved into the fast lane of living and poverty had brought his lifestyle to a screeching halt. How could he have fallen from being an honored son of a wealthy landowner to being ravished with hunger in a pigpen?

Fortunately this desperation brought him to his senses and to the point of repentance. He had left home in a highly decorated robe, showing his prestige, but now he was dressed only in filthy rags. Focusing on home, he left the pigpen to trudge the long road back to where he'd come from.

Shame, humiliation and repentance all vied for his attention. What was he to expect? Would his father even look at him after his blatant defiance? As he neared home, his questions were all answered in a moment.

Though the son was thin, ragged and filthy, the ever-watchful father recognized his prodigal at a distance. Running with open arms, he embraced the frail form before him. He brought the best meil-type robe and put it on him, placing a ring on his finger and shoes on his feet. A feast was prepared, and there was merriment in the home!

The father's love and gladness were clearly seen by all those in the house!

Though we have gone astray as this prodigal had, our heavenly Father has His robe of righteousness, a symbolic and spiritual robe, waiting for us. He too is just waiting for our return to Him with a repentant attitude so He can present us with our fresh new attire, our robe of righteousness, Christ.

I MADE MY ROBE OF RIGHTEOUSNESS A PERSONAL DECISION

"Oh, I feel like traveling on...my Heavenly home is bright and fair, and I feel like traveling on," were words that rang in the back of the old VW bus as it headed down Highway 22 toward a small burg in Iowa. As a group of newly liberated Christians, we were jubilant as we traveled the thirty miles to a pond for a baptismal service.

After my parent's excommunication from our former denomination, my family visited various churches throughout our area. I was exposed to many different forms of worship without understanding about Christ's redemption and how it applied to me. As my brother and I entered our teens, my parents decided it was time to put down church roots and moved us back to the state of my birth, Iowa.

At the age of fifteen, after completing the catechism classes of a more liberal branch of our former denomination, I ceremoniously had some water poured on my head and assumed I had obtained my salvation. Meanwhile, God remained hidden from me behind man-made ordinances. I believed that to transgress these traditions would send me directly to Hell, and yet my self-righteousness was unfulfilling.

After a few years of spiritual faltering and unfulfilled yearnings my family was exposed to the miraculous move of the Holy Spirit in our area. At the time God graciously filled me with His Spirit, the eyes of my understanding were opened to faith in Christ's finished work on Calvary. I realized that He completed all I needed to obtain His righteousness.

Up until this time I had been haunted by the fact that I couldn't pinpoint an exact date of my salvation. As we sang God's praises in the back of that old clattering bus, I knew that this baptism would provide me with a date and time of public confession of my new birth. Christ's work was completed on Calvary, and I had taken the step of identifying with His death, burial and resurrection! I determined never again to question my salvation.

YOU MUST MAKE YOUR SALVATION A PERSONAL MATTER

Through my studies of scripture I have come to the understanding that the words soul, heart and spirit are often used interchangeably and may be difficult to distinguish from each other unless we search out their root meanings. In order to simplify this study, I have chosen to use this three-point formula to help you understand what I am talking about.

1. We are spirit

We know that God is a Spirit, but we may seldom think of ourselves as spirit beings also. Nevertheless, it is our spirit-man that is the real 'us'. When God breathed the breath of life into Adam, He breathed his eternalness into human form, thus distinguishing us from the rest of His creation. It is the eternal part of humanity that Christ came to redeem and which must have a personal relationship with God. We indeed are spirit. (See Genesis 1:26; 5:1)

2. We live in a body

Although the physical body is not the main emphasis of this study we are told in I Corinthians 3:16, 17 that we are God's temple. I urge you to study this Scripture which also gives strong warning against defiling or bringing to a worse state this temple of God. I Corinthians 6:19 declares that our body is the temple of the Holy Ghost and that we are to honor Him with our bodies.

God has given me personal convictions about our 'junk food' habits. God wants us to exercise properly, remain active and nourish our bodies with the best possible foods. Even though a 'sit down meal' with the family is nearly a lost art in our society, it is still a healthy way of life. It does more than just nourishing the physical body, but lends to building relationships as well.

Even though we know that when we leave this earth this mortal flesh will put on immortality and will change these bodies into incorruptible bodies, we need not hasten the process by not caring for the body (I Corinthians 15:53,54).

In the resurrection we will get our new bodies automatically if our spirit man is clothed with God's robe of righteousness. This understanding allows us to be wise in caring for our bodies, while providing the space we need to care for our first priorities, our spirit and then our soul.

3. We have a soul

Our soul is made up of three components: our mind (or intellect), our will and our emotions (or feelings). Our soul is what creates our habits. Good habits are formed when they have the spiritual component of the heart in alignment with God's Word.

The following chapters will deal largely with the aspects of the soul, but before we can go there we must take care of our spiritual state. In order to do this we must understand that we inherited a sin nature which we must repent of (I Corinthian 15:45). Romans 3:23 plainly declares that we have all sinned and fallen short of God's glory and honor of which He is worthy.

Although I have just pointed out that we all have a sinful nature that we need to repent of we also have a solid foundation of love to rely on. Read the following passage and feel the love that God has for you. John 3:16 declares, *"For God so loved the world that He gave His only begotten Son, that whoever believes in Him should not perish but have everlasting life."*

This means that God, in His infinite love, offers us redemption through His only begotten Son, Jesus Christ. God did this so that Christ might die on the cross for us and become the Savior of the world. Christ being God in human form was the only One who could take onto Himself the form of a servant and be made sin for us. (Philippians 2:7, 8)

If you have never repented of your sins and asked Jesus to come and redeem you, now is the time for you to move beyond your old past and invite Him into your life. Maybe you have asked Him to be your Savior and have not made Him your Lord. If so, then I also invite you to pray the following prayer. Perhaps you are someone who asked Christ into your life a long time ago but you have been swayed away by various things in life; then you too must come and kneel with me. Visualize the foot of the cross of Christ where His blood was shed for the cleansing of all our sins.

If you are one who has already invited Jesus into your heart, then reaffirm that relationship. If you have questioned your salvation, do this in faith and remember the date so you'll never again question the condition of your spirit man. If you have never heard of God's gift of redemption, or if you have never asked Jesus to personally come into your life, now is your time!

As you read this example prayer, make it your own. You must do more than just read it. Make it the cry of your heart. Insert your personal repentance, your own willfulness and your individual acceptance of God's precious gift of His love to you.

Dear precious Father in Heaven,

I come to you now as the prodigal son did when he returned to his father. I come with a contrite heart because I realize that I have sinned. I understand that I have denied Your grace and wasted Your substance. Forgive me for my sins. I repent of these and choose to turn away from them.

I believe that Jesus, Your Son, shed his blood and died on the cross for the redemption and purification of my spirit. I accept the forgiveness that You have for me, and I enter into Your kingdom by the authority of that divine sacrifice. I know that I am now free to move beyond the law of sin and death and that I am a new creature in Christ Jesus.

Thank You for washing my sins away. Thank You for giving me an entrance into Your kingdom. I now believe that I receive my symbolic robe that is Your righteousness. I am now one of Your own beloved children. Lead me, guide me and help me to grow in You and Your Word.

Thank you for Your free gift of salvation. I receive it now and make You the Savior and Lord of my life.

I take that salvation, and rise up and walk in faith that Christ's robe of righteousness is my source of strength. As Peter walked on the water, so have You enabled me to walk in life. I trust that I will become victorious in my life here on earth, because of what Your Son has done for me.

In Jesus' name I pray, Amen.

Now that you have prayed this prayer of rededication, or as a first time prayer, it is important that you sign and date your commitment as a reminder of your decision to accept His plan of salvation. Please do so by hand writing the prayer as you prayed it on separate piece of paper, then sign and date the prayer to record is forever for yourself.

AN ILLUSTRATION FOR CLARIFICATION

Following Jesus' example of using parables, I'll use an illustration to help you relate what you did when you prayed the sinner's prayer.

Two-year-old Joel was the only son of millionaires Mike and Nancy. Mike owned several businesses in various states, and Nancy was the mistress of their lavish estate. Nancy and Mike both adored their son and worked hard to equip him with all the material possessions that he would ever need. Nancy's schedule often took her out of the home, but a very capable staff was left in charge at home.

One blustery winter night after a promotional banquet, Mike and Nancy headed home from the convention center in hopes of arriving in time to tuck Joel into bed. The winds had worsened, and icy snow blurred their vision as they rounded a curve. Suddenly their car went into a spin and down a steep embankment. It took several hours to release them from the wreckage and get them into the local intensive care unit. Though they were in critical condition, they summoned their lawyer. There, in their feeble state, they finalized the papers they'd been working on to name their infant son the heir to all their possessions.

Soon after the accident Joel found himself orphaned and heir to all his parents' wealth. There were, however, clauses in the will that kept Joel from being able to access his inheritance until he had successfully finished certain requirements in school and until he turned twenty-one. He was given guardians, the best teachers, and all that he needed during his years of maturing, and yet he was totally unable to access the businesses of his late father or liquidate the estate of his parents.

When Joel reached the age and level of maturity that his parents had required of him on their deathbeds, he stepped into the realm of activating and managing his own inheritance.

You have prayed the sinner's prayer and have stepped into your spiritual inheritance, much of which you will not be able to activate in an immature spiritual state. Since this is the case you may be asking, "What really happened when I prayed and asked Jesus to be my Savior and Lord?"

It is true that you still have the same past, the same debts to pay and house payments to make. You still have the same mother-in-law, the same abusive father, the same siblings or the same bratty children. Whatever your case may be up to this point, you still have your past. That will not change, but what has changed is YOU!

You are now saved from the eternal damnation of hell. You have come by the authority of Christ Jesus to obtain your salvation. (See Acts 4:12)

You are now in a spiritual position where Jesus walks beside you. You no longer need to give in to the old sinful habits.

According to Romans 6:14 sin no longer has dominion over you. The thing that has changed is that you are no longer a subject of sin. You are justified, that is to be 'just-as-if-I'd-never-sinned'. Because of what Jesus did when he died on the cross and rose again, you are given spiritual authority to overcome the vices of sin.

You have all the promises of God left to you and are in the process of maturing spiritually. By taking this step of faith you have joined Joseph in appropriating your robe of righteousness. Even as Joel's inheritance papers had been written and signed, so have your redemption papers been completed. You must now go on and mature fully to be a completed work in Christ.

YOU ARE NOW WEARING GOD'S MEIL COAT

The clothing the descendants of Abraham wore was significant to portray position, identification and feelings. The highest-ranking officers of the Hebrews wore the colorful, long-sleeved coat referred to as the meil robe. It signified a position of importance and high esteem.[3]

Revelation 1:6 tells us that our spiritual position in God's kingdom is also one that demands respect. *"And has made us kings and priests unto His God and Father; to Him be glory and dominion for ever and ever, Amen."*

In Revelation 5:10 God reaffirms this: *"And have made us kings and priests to our God and we shall reign on the earth."*

The prophet Isaiah had insight into this truth before Christ was born. In Isaiah 61:10 he says, *"I will greatly rejoice in the LORD, my soul shall be joyful in my God: For he hath clothed me with the garments of salvation, he hath covered me with the robe of righteousness, as a bridegroom decks himself with ornaments, and as a bride adorns herself with her jewels."*

By this concept we're challenged to allow this symbolic meil-type robe become our new identification and way of thinking. The journey through Joseph's lifetime and actual changes of garments will move us beyond the bondages of our old life without Christ.

WHAT YOU HAVE DONE

You have allowed Joseph to become your example of righteousness received by faith.

You have prayed the sinner's prayer, asking Jesus to come into your heart and making His righteousness your own personal possession.

You have signed and dated your prayer so you will never forget your commitment and go back to the old life.

You have accessed the spiritually legal port of entrance into the Kingdom of God; giving you rights to claim every promise God has ever spoken to, by or about you.

By this beginning of a new lifestyle and thought patterns you have denied all rights to sin and to Satan.

You have received the forgiveness of your sins which renders your spirit-man spotless in the eyes of God.

You have stepped past the old enslaved you, and are now a blessed child of the Everlasting Heavenly Father!

AN EXERCISE TO PRACTICE

Now having legal access to every promise of God, you know sin no longer has dominion over you. To help you understand just what has happened to you I want you to turn to Romans chapter six in your Bible (Romans is the sixth book in the New Testament). As you read this chapter, I want you to personalize it by exchanging each *"we"* with the personal pronoun *'I'*, and then add your name. For example, I would read the first verse like this:

"What shall I, Lydia, say then? Shall I, Lydia, continue in sin that grace may abound?"

Each time you come to a place that you want to doubt your salvation, return to this chapter and make it your personal affirmation. Understand that sin now has no more dominion over you. You are free to choose a Godly lifestyle, freed from sin by God's grace. Enjoy your freedom to choose what's right!

CHAPTER TWO

The Coat of Many Colors

~ *Genesis 37:1-11* ~

*D*o you ever find yourself wishing there was someone who would love you unconditionally and without restraint? Well, I have exciting news for you!

The coat of many colors that Jacob made for his favorite son, Joseph, is symbolic of God's love to each of us. Though Jacob's natural love was imperfect, God's supernatural love is unconditional, without partiality and perfect toward His children. If you forget everything else that you read in *Beyond the Colorful Coat*, never forget the great love God has for you. You have taken Jesus as your Savior, and you now belong to His family. He loves you more than any earthly father ever loved a child. His love for us does not mean that He will always choose the easiest path for us. It does mean that He loves us enough to walk with us through our trials. We will see this great love unfold as we journey on with Joseph.

God and love cannot be separated from each other, for "*God is love*". (I John 4:8). Spiros Zodhiates, Ph.D., in *The Complete Word Study Dictionary of the New Testament,* defines the words 'love' or 'agape': "It is God's willful direction toward man. It involves God doing what He knows is best for man and not necessarily what man desires."

Spiros Zodhiates further explains this by using John 3:16 for an example of God's love in sending us His Son, Jesus Christ. Jesus was not what the world wanted, but He was what we all needed. God's love is His very nature. It is His character, His divine sovereignty, and His complete being.[1]

JACOB FAVORS JOSEPH

Jacob had moved his family to Hebron, the place God had promised to give his grandfather, Abraham. Even though Hebron lay in a shallow valley, it was about 3,000 feet above sea level and about 4,300 feet above the Dead Sea that lay just a few miles to the east. It was situated 19 miles South-West of Jerusalem on the main road that leads southward to Beer-sheba.[2] It is here in Hebron that we will watch the following story unfold.

A week earlier Jacob had sent his older sons to Beersheba to herd his sheep. Now, as was typical for Jacob, he summons Joseph saying, "Here, Joseph, take these fresh baked loaves of bread and this cheese and go see how your brothers are doing. As you pass others along the way, find out if your brothers have been in the area and be sure to bring the details of their whereabouts back to me."

Even though Joseph is approaching his seventeenth birthday, his father still instructs him as a child, "You should be able to find your brothers before nightfall. You may sleep with them in the field tonight, but be sure you're back before dark tomorrow night."

The next day Jacob is anxious for his son to return home safely and paces impatiently in front of his tent door as he scans the horizon with keen eyes. Jacob's eagerness for his son's return not only hinges on anxiety but also on excitement. He has spent many hours in making a special coat for Joseph that would mark him with honor and rank. It is most likely the *meil-type* robe that marked a man as the chief or heir.[3] It is probable that the many colors come from the intricate needlework that is stitched into it.

Jacob knows his other sons will understand that he means for Joseph to be the head of the tribe or to be over them. He also knows it is going against the customary practice of having the firstborn become his heir. It seems that Jacob isn't taking to heart the fact that his other sons will hate both him, for making the coat, and their half-brother for wearing it.

There is no Biblical record that Joseph had done anything to merit the coat of many colors. Wisdom would have taught Jacob to allow God to promote Joseph in His time; however, tunnel vision prompts this premature promotion.

As the sun dips closer and closer to the western horizon spreading a pink film across the rolling hills, Jacob finally spots the speck on the southern landscape he was looking for. Having the finished coat of many colors in hand, he hurries to meet his son.

Joseph first feels concern when he sees his father hurriedly coming to meet him; but his concern quickly changes to surprise when he was close enough to hear his father.

"Happy Birthday, Joseph!" Jacob exclaimed jovially, "I have made a coat of many colors for you. This coat will set you apart and above your brothers. All who see you will know that I have honored you as the head of my sons."

Joseph is breathless as he takes the beautiful garment from his father and pulls it on. "Oh, Father, this is lovely, and a perfect fit!" Joseph cries with delight.

"I'll always wear this distinguished identification and people will know I am the honored son." Joseph's pride is heightened another notch as he struts about wearing his prized possession.

After the hugs and embraces are over and the excitement has died down a bit, Jacob asks Joseph about his other sons. Joseph had listened to conversations and brought back evil reports about his brothers' deeds. At his father's prompting, he had become an expert at telling on his brothers.

Do you realize that unearned or premature favor often leads to favoritism and drives a sharp wedge into relationships? As this story unfolds we will see this happen because of Jacob's deliberate favoritism shown to Joseph.

Try to imagine the shock the ten big brothers have the first time they see Joseph parading in his robe, identifying him as their chief. Fighting and arguments break out as the brothers angrily address Joseph. Jacob quietly stands by and watches from a distance. He justifies his deeds by the love he had for Rachel's firstborn.

GOD GIVES DREAMS TO JOSEPH

Though Joseph's humanity is showing by the unwise agreements he has become entangled with, God gives him two dreams. Without realizing it at the time these dreams foretell the promotion of his future, and reinforce the love God has for him.

It is too early in the morning even for shepherds to be awakened out under the canopy of twinkling stars, but Joseph won't restrain himself. "Hey brothers," I can hear him boast, "Listen to this dream I had."

"Hush, child. I want to finish my sleep," Simeon demands.

"I can't be quiet, brothers! This is the most exciting dream I have ever dreamed!" Joseph continues.

"A dream can't be that important," groans Naphtali into his shepherd's robe.

The brothers, as you or I would, hate to have their sleep disturbed but Joseph wouldn't wait until his brothers awaken. "Okay, listen-up, you guys. See if you can get back to sleep after I tell you this dream. It was so vivid and so clear! I felt the autumn sun brush against my cheeks and I remember the aroma of our freshly-cut wheat. The wheat's golden shine made me feel like a wealthy man. The stalks felt smooth in my hands as I grabbed arms full and stacked them into sheaves."

"Oh, be quiet, dreamer," Gad exclaims. "You must have eaten too much porridge last night! Indigestion can do that, you know. Now hush, I've heard enough!"

"I know it's early, but you've got to hear the rest of my dream," Joseph continues. "I dreamed that we were all out in the field binding the wheat into sheaves. We each had our own sheaves, and as we stood them upright yours all bowed down to mine! You tried to get yours to stand upright, but they always bowed in my direction. I can't wait to tell Papa!"

The strutting youth, with his coat of many colors, is not careful to consider the sacredness of God's revelation to him. He knows the dream is of God, but rather than laying it before God and praying that He would bring it to fulfillment, Joseph broadcasts it wherever possible.

A few nights later Joseph has another dream, but this time not only the eleven stars bow to his star, but the moon and the sun bow also. Again Joseph boasts that God has given him a full-colored dream. The brothers are outraged and start plotting to rid themselves of the dreamer.

The brothers, painfully aware of their father's fondness of Joseph, become more jealous as they realize God is also affirming their little brother. They rebel against this fact, causing the home front to become a chaotic place of sibling rivalry and disturbances.

DIVINELY FORTIFIED LOVE

My friend, Inis, has often told me, "Never question in the dark what God has shown you in the light." When God speaks He floods our understanding with spiritual light, however, before these God-given messages can be fulfilled they must be tried.

You have just given your heart to the Lord and now you may find your faith being tested. When we're in the middle of chaos most of us find ourselves questioning God's love and may wonder if He even exists or cares about us.

As we move further into the life of Joseph, we will see that God was there all the time. Joseph had two powerful visitations from God. He had promises to look forward to, but with the tests of time, they seemingly disappear into the maze of life.

God loved Joseph so much He stepped in to deliver him from any and every element stemming from his own unregenerated soul. God planned that Joseph's mind, will and emotions agree with what He promised him. God had to use 'tough love' to bring this to fulfillment.

The principles of God's divine love apply to our lives as well. We may not have had the full-colored dreams that Joseph had, but we need to realize that God loves us equally and speaks a word of affirmation to us from Jeremiah 31:3.

> *"The LORD has appeared of old to me, saying, 'Yes, I have loved you with an everlasting love: Therefore with loving kindness I have drawn you.'"*

When God speaks as directly to His people as He did to Joseph, it is of utmost importance that we remember and make note of what He has said. Because of God's love for us, He will test that word before He fulfills it. If we don't embrace it through faith it will not withstand the refiner's fire.

The challenge is to realize and embrace God's love for us. Responding according the Scriptures will build our faith during our refining process, enabling us to move forward into the full benefit of His love.

GOD ALWAYS SPEAKS INTO OUR FUTURE

Have you ever had a promise from God that you felt was personally yours but then it just didn't materialize?

The reason is usually because we expect the promise to be immediate. In our fast-paced society it is difficult for us to develop our faith. We wake up with instant coffee, we drive in the fast lane of traffic and we expect immediate responses to our dreams or demands. We don't want any waiting lines in the supermarket, and we don't want to get stuck in back of the airplane or even have to wait for a senior citizen in the crosswalk.

In Joseph's case, he had to wait twenty-two years to see his dreams fulfilled. Moses was tested for forty years. He spent those years herding Jethro's sheep on the backside of the desert before he became the deliverer for Israel (Acts 7:30). Even Jesus had to wait to fulfill His ministry on earth (Luke 2:51).

God doesn't give His promises for the past 'us' or the present 'us,' but to the transformed 'us'. God can fulfill the dreams He gives when our natural man becomes a reflection of Christ. There will always be a refining process that He has to bring us through in order to fulfill His plan for us. By giving Joseph dreams, God gave him promises about his future. Joseph was like many of us are: he didn't know that the fulfillment of the dreams would be far down a long journey of years.

You see, Joseph had embarked on a journey of faith, but that faith was untested. He had been given dreams of promise, but their fulfillment was not for the immediate time frame. It was for his future. There is no doubt that he had passion to see his dreams fulfilled but his passion wasn't channeled. The favor bestowed on him by his father was given prematurely. And though there was the gold of God's presence in Joseph's life, that gold was unrefined.

When my husband and I moved to Wisconsin from San Antonio, God had given me two identical, full-color dreams in which I saw a place I recognized in this area. I saw two women running toward me, as if in a slow-motion video. I expected these women to immediately be in my life, but it took years for the dream to be fulfilled. Meanwhile I didn't respond to my unexpected situation according to faith. Instead I reacted according to the reasoning of my own mind. I gave in to my negative emotions rather than pray in the fulfillment of my dreams. I am grateful to God for His grace to me. After several years of testing, the dreams were fulfilled and God brought these ladies into my life.

Though God speaks into our future, He always speaks words of love to each of us. We may face years of refinement before we see the promises fulfilled but if we respond to His everlasting love according to His commands, we will obtain their fulfillment.

IT LITERALLY TAKES GOD TO FULFILL HIS PROMISE

As I have studied the life of Joseph, I sense that he did some things in his own boastful way to fulfill the dreams he had. Being human, he didn't realize the power of prayer that was available to him. He was young, inexperienced and naive as he gloated over his dreams and flaunted his colorful coat.

Symbolically he was wearing the robe that represents God's righteousness which he had obtained by faith, yet he still allowed elements of his mind, will, and emotions to rule him. No matter how hard Joseph might have tried to fulfill his own dreams, only God could have fulfilled them.

I love what the apostle Paul says in Philippians 1:6: *"being confident of this very thing, that He who has begun a good work in you will complete it until the day of Jesus Christ;"* Then in Philippians 2:13 he reaffirms this truth: *"for it is God who works in you both to will and to do for His good pleasure."*

Mary, the mother of Jesus, had a visitor, the angel Gabriel. He told her not to fear for she would bear the Son conceived by the Holy Spirit. Nobody had ever had a more awesome visitation than Mary's, but she kept the thing in her heart and didn't even tell her fiancé about the visit. Later when the shepherds came and told of their visit by the multitude of angels, she again pondered their message in her heart (Luke 2:19).

It takes a mature Christian to understand the truth of I Thessalonians 5:24: *"He who calls you is faithful, who also will do it."* This marvelous scripture assures us that God will do what He says He will do.

We will see as we move onward in this study of the life of Joseph that our own will has to be dealt with as we pass through God's refining process. In the age we're living, parents are now afraid to discipline their children. This is one reason why it's difficult for us to understanding that God disciplines us BECAUSE He loves us.

GOD SPEAKS ABOUT REFINEMENT

Hebrews 12:11 clarifies this truth. *"Now no chastening seems to be joyful for the present, but painful; nevertheless, afterward it yields the peaceable fruit of righteousness to those who have been trained by it."*

We have free access to the concept of God's 'tough love' through the Scriptures. Our friend Joseph is an excellent example of such an experience.

Read with me Hebrews 12:5b-6: *"My son, do not despise the chastening of the LORD, Nor be discouraged when you are rebuked by Him: For whom the LORD loves He chastens, and scourges every son whom He receives."*

I Peter 1:6,7: *"{You should} be exceedingly glad on this account, though now for a little while you may be distressed by trials and suffer temptations, so that [the genuineness] of your faith*

may be tested, [your faith] which is infinitely more precious than
the perishable gold which is tested and purified by fire. [This
proving of your faith is intended] to redound to [your] praise and
glory and honor when Jesus Christ (the Messiah, the Anointed
One) is revealed.* (Amplified Bible)

Job 5:17: *"Behold, happy is the man whom God corrects;
Therefore do not despise the chastening of the Almighty."*

There are many elements in the lives of believers which work
together to help our process of refinement. If we don't humbly
yield to God's procedures to refine us, we take long detours on our
own journey into God's destiny. The more we avail ourselves to
these principles and precepts, the sooner the Lord can fulfill His
promises and promote us to our positions of spiritual authority.

GOD'S LOVE TO US DEMANDS A RESPONSE FROM US

Do you remember when you first fell in love with your spouse?
You sought for any moments you could scrape together to convey
your love to him or her. You wanted to spend time together, share
your hopes and dreams, and you made personal adjustments to be
compatible with the one you loved.

In this modern society many have taken on the "What about
me?" attitude. In too many cases it is no longer a natural thing to
automatically respond to the love of another. Yet this is God's plan
and His desire. He has no ulterior motive when He disciplines those
He loves. He does this to bring us to Himself.

How is it that we so often take God's love for granted when He
loves us like no other? Could it be that we have not understood or
responded correctly to His love?

The key to the response God expects from us is found in Jesus' words in Matthew 22:37-40. This is the portion of Scripture that we call "the golden rule." I call it one of my "bottom-line" Scriptures because it uses the word "all" four times. All is an absolute concept. There are no stragglers; there is no straying, and no diversion in the word "all." It is unadulterated, undiluted and indefectible in its concept. "All" is all-inclusive!

Verses 37-38 command, *"'You shall love the LORD your God with all your heart, with all your soul, and with all your mind.' This is the first and great commandment..."*

The person is wise who remembers that in order to receive God's love, he or she must totally respond to it. As we continue to journey through Joseph's life and move beyond the symbolism of his seven various garments, we will see clearly how to respond to His love.

When you think of Joseph's robe of many colors, let it remind you that God loves you unconditionally and eternally.

WHAT YOU HAVE LEARNED

Jacob played favorites and bestowed premature favor on his most loved son, Joseph.

God honored Joseph with two dreams foretelling his future.

God loves us with an everlasting love.

It takes God's painfully refining process to fulfill the vision He gives.

Our response to God's love must be to love Him with all our heart, our soul, our strength and our mind.

While God chastens and rebukes us, He says that the trying of our faith is more precious than gold that perishes.

AN EXERCISE TO PRACTICE

Copy Romans 8:35-39 onto a 3x5 card to carry with you to help you memorize the verses. Be sure to use a version of the Bible that clarifies God's love for you. My personally preference is the King James Version.

Dothan and the Refining Process

~ Genesis 37:12-27 ~

C ome along" Joseph calls to us as he heads northward with provisions for his brothers. The early morning breeze rustles through his dark hair and his colorful coat catches the rays of the early sunshine. The exuberance of youth compels him back to Shechem, one of the places of his childhood. Sometime earlier his father had sent the brothers on the 18-mile trek to find pasture for their sheep, and now Joseph was sent, as usual, to check on their well-being.

Joseph's pride in his most prized possession, his elaborate coat, spurs him along his journey. Having traveled in those parts earlier in his life, he begins his journey to Shechem without concern. However, unbeknownst to Joseph, the brothers had left the area earlier and he now becomes disorientated in his search. A man of that region finds him wandering in the fields.

"You must be the younger son of Jacob," the man says.

"Yes, I am and I'm coming to check on my brothers. Do you know where they are?" Joseph asks.

The man who found him is very helpful, telling him that he had overheard the brothers talk of moving another thirteen miles farther north to Dothan.

As Joseph heads toward the hill that marks Dothan, the man calls after him, "Your brothers won't have a hard time spotting you since you're wearing that brightly colored coat that I've heard them talk about."

The man is right. The brothers, being seasoned shepherds, have eagle-eyes and are able to spot danger at a distance. But this time it isn't danger that they spot. It's the brother they're jealous of. It's Joseph.

"Here comes the dreamer!" Naphtali calls to his brothers as he remembers the early morning accounts by Joseph, which had awakened and angered him.

"Hey, this is our opportunity!" I can hear another say.

Levi sneers, "We are so far from home that Father will never know what happened to the tattle-tale when he never shows up on his doorstep again!" The brothers explode in laughter!

"It's not fair that Father should give this special honor to our little brother," says Simeon, one of Leah's older sons. "We'll be justified in getting rid of our half-brother. Father favors him just because he loved Joseph's mother more than he ever loved ours. He hasn't done a thing to earn this coat of many colors and the significance it bears. Let's take that coat away from him."

By the time Joseph reaches the setting where the sheep are grazing peacefully, the brothers' hearts have filled with the rages of hatred and murder. Their plan is to rip up his coat, dip it in goat's blood and take it to their father as 'evidence' of Joseph's death. "That will serve our dad right for playing favorites," they all agree.

"Give me back my coat! You can't do this to me!" Joseph pleads with a look of betrayal on his face. But his pleas are to no avail because the vast open spaces are the only ears that heed his appeals. His brothers' hearts are calloused and cold.

He screams frantically as the brothers plot to kill him, "Someone help me! Can anyone hear me?" The vastness of the countryside cannot produce an answer. He soon realizes how useless it is to waste his energy calling for help when his brothers are gloating over their good fortune.

Just as the brothers prepare to throw stones at him, Reuben comes to Joseph's rescue. "Instead of killing Joseph, let's throw him into this empty well." The oldest brother secretly hopes to deliver Joseph back to his father.

Later, while Reuben is off herding sheep, the rest of the clan decides to sell Joseph to a caravan of Midianite merchants headed into Egypt.

Papyri, ancient documents, manuscripts, or scrolls used by the Egyptians, Greeks and Romans indicate that slaves from Palestine during that age were prized possessions for an Egyptian. According to history these merchants were carrying loads of spices for embalming, so a young handsome Canaanite slave would be a good addition to their cargo.

The brothers settle for the minimum price for a slave and sell him for only 20 pieces of silver, which in today's economy would be the equivalent of only $15.00. This price affords each of the gloating brothers two seventy-five cent silver pieces to pocket.[1]

IS THIS THE END?

Joseph, stripped bare, is shackled and begins the trek into Egypt without any sympathy from his cruel brothers. There are no last good-byes and Joseph's tears are the only ones shed at the parting.

It all seems so final! He finds himself on an unplanned journey of approximately 300 miles. When he had left his father's house at dawn, this change in circumstances was totally unexpected. It was a turn in the road that he certainly hadn't desired. But there wasn't a thing he could do to direct or stop this journey into Egypt.

The story that started out with the brilliant colors of promise seems to be ending in total defeat, defying circumstances and an unfulfilled vision! Is this actually the crushed remains of Joseph's dreams? At this point in his life Joseph seemed to be unidentified, unknown, unimportant and unloved—a 'nobody' lost in the wilderness. He may well have been wondering if this trip would lead to his death. Would Joseph find anything worth living for beyond the borders of Canaan, in the land of idolatry and witchcraft? Would the faith of his forefathers prevail on his way into Egypt?

MY PAIN WAS MIXED WITH JOSEPH'S

It was at this point of reading Joseph's story that I actually begin writing these lessons on his life. I was doing my Bible reading and as I read this portion in Genesis chapter 37. I wept for Joseph. I felt the anguish in his circumstances because of the times I've felt rejected by friends and misunderstood by peers. The tears for my own pain seemed to blend with Joseph's. I was touched with compassion for him and understood his desperation. As I cried I asked, "What had the poor lad done to get himself into such trouble?" You see, it was through the various times of deep pain in my own life that I started to learn about God's healing grace and love. I have had glimpses of God's desire to change me until I no longer felt my pain in the light of Calvary's pain.

After serving as missionaries in the Philippines for eight years, our family returned to the States at a time I thought was premature. Things had happened in, to, and through our family that God longed to reconcile. God begin teaching me to utilize the pain of that experience to appropriate changes for my own life. He used these types of experiences to teach me that Godly character far exceeds the importance of an honored position. The pain I felt back then has served to bring me through barriers of my own unsurrendered soul and into God's loving embrace. These tests taught me that God wasn't ending His call on my life; instead He was giving me the beginning of a new understanding regarding His call in my life.

I knew from experience that the infliction of unmerited injustice in the life of the believer is for the purpose of refinement and transformation. It has nothing to do with God changing His mind about us or His call in our lives. He never purposes our tests to crush the dreams He's given.

Even though I had seen bits and pieces of God's desire to change me before writing the lessons He was showing me through this study on the life of Joseph, I was very reluctant to write what I was seeing. I realized that Joseph was an Old Testament type of Jesus, and I was unwilling to paint him as needing to make changes and adjustment in His own life. If I were to portray him as being imperfect and needing to change, than surely I would need to allow God to make changes in my own life.

It was not until I came to Hebrews 5:8 and read that Jesus, the Son of God, learned obedience through suffering that I relented and said, "Lord, change me. I will write the lessons you give me to write."

At that point I didn't know it would be a book I'd be writing, but rather that He wanted to transform me into having the same mindset as Christ had.

The journey of writing this message hasn't brought me great earthly honor, for it is a message that demands change in the hearts of the believer. In the same way, God was not as excited about Joseph being exalted to an honorable position as He was in building His own character in Joseph's life. God had called him to project His own attributes of God-likeness through him.

JOSEPH HAD HIS CROSS TO BEAR

Cross-bearing is never easy for any of us, but it is necessary for all who will follow the Lord. Paul was challenged by the example of the Savior's cross bearing. He calls this process of carrying our cross *"fellow of his suffering"*.

Who would desire to fellowship with suffering? It is not what we like, but it is what we need. As we continue our acquaintance with Joseph's transformation we will see that there had to be the beginning of the embracing of God's grace. This grace converts him into one of Scripture's greatest examples of God-given dreams fulfilled.

With the desert sand stinging the young captive's bare back and with the brutal sun unleashing it's fury upon Joseph there was a seed of faith being planted. Through Joseph's tears I can see him humming Thomas Shepherd's ancient hymn, written in 1693.

> Must Jesus bear the cross alone,
> And all the world go free?
> No, there's a cross for ev'ryone,
> And there's a cross for me.

> The consecrated cross I'll bear,
> Till death shall set me free,
> And then go on a crown to wear,
> For there's a crown for me.

Just a few verses of song bring a pin-point of hope to Joseph. Somehow he knows that he must remember the God of his fathers. Even though Joseph is crying, he is singing the last verse. Let us listen in and sing with him.

> O precious cross! O glorious crown!
> O resurrection day!
> Ye angels, from the stars come down,
> And bear my soul away.

Chances are that we, like Joseph, are not at the end, but at the mere beginnings of walking the path to having our dreams fulfilled. This was only the end of the colorful coat, but by no means the end of Joseph's unfulfilled dreams.

THE SONG OF FAITH OR THE SONG OF VICTORY

Many of us sing praises after the test has passed. We call this the song of victory. Such was the case with Moses and the children of Israel at the crossing of the Red sea found in Exodus chapters 14 and 15. In Exodus 14:10-12 the Israelites were greatly afraid and cried to the Lord. Then they accused Moses of bringing them out to kill them in the wilderness. They declared that it would have been better for them to have stayed in Egypt and remained slaves under the cruelty of the Pharaoh.

We see that Moses had to still them and tell them not to fear. He promised that they would see their salvation through the power of God. He also promised that the Egyptians who were pursuing them would never be seen again. In verse 14 he says, *"The Lord will fight for you and you shall hold your peace."*

God commanded the people to go forward as Moses stretched out his rod over the Red Sea. As he did this the waters were divided by a strong east wind. The wind dried up the sea and the children of Israel marched forward through the dried-up sea bed all that night. God guided them with a supernatural light.

In Exodus 15 we can read the beautiful song of victory that the children of Israel sang after the test. Although this is a beautiful song of deliverance and worship, it could have been a song of faith as they faced the test of the Egyptians pursuing behind them and the Red Sea in front of them.

Before we went to the Philippines my pastor's wife told me to keep singing my songs of worship when things were difficult. As I look back now I repent that this was not what I did in many instances. I am still learning to sing the songs of faith in the face of misunderstanding, heartaches and various other trials.

My greatest earthly example of someone who always sang her songs of faith is my late mother. I have an ideal pattern of this as I visualize my mother adoring Jesus in heaven. Her song is now one of victory, but for decades it was a song of faith.

It is the meditation of our heart, the song that we sing and the faith we express through worship that compels us to move beyond the here and now. Although I am not aware that Scripture records any Psalms of Joseph, we can easily avail ourselves to David's many Psalms. These Psalms are God's Word, His Word is for the generations past to the eternity to come.

WHAT YOU HAVE LEARNED

God started Joseph's process of refinement at Dothan.

Joseph was stripped of his identity and sold into Egypt by his brothers.

Godly character far exceeds the importance of honored position

In the natural it looked like there was no way for God to fulfill the dreams He had given to Joseph

Joseph was stripped of his identification and on a road that seemed to lead to nowhere

Tiny glimmers of faith and hope gave him enough courage to hum during times of his distress

It is of more importance to sing a song of faith before the battle is won than to sing the song of victory after the answer has been given

AN EXERCISE TO PRACTICE

Take your Bible to a quiet place. Find the book of Psalm right in the middle of the Bible and begin to sing those Psalms to God. Psalm 100 could be a good place to start. Singing it over and over will help you memorize it and store it in your spirit.

There are many beautiful Psalms of praise to God. Read the whole book and write on a 3x5 card a few verses you want to learn to sing and meditate on. God with give you a tune if you ask Him to, or you can just start singing your own tune. Do not be ashamed because God will be the only one listening. He is listening to the motives in your heart and not the sound of your voice.

CHAPTER FOUR

Transition of the Soul

~ Romans 12:1, 2 ~

*T*he Midianite merchants who had struck a slick bargain when they bought Joseph from his brothers realized they had a treasure on their hands. Because of this they brought him through the wilderness, the deserts, drought and pits, always protecting him from harm. Generally we don't think about it in this way, but Joseph has been kept in safety in the pit until the perfect time for his release and sale to the Midianite merchants. Though it is unlikely that he recognized his experience in the pit as God's place of preservation for His exact time of his release, as we search deeper into his life we will see this is exactly the plan of God.

Here he again is unable to see how he is being preserved on this undesired journey—a journey that will lead him into the land where he'll experience further captivity. On this voyage we will follow the footprints of transition that the triumphing Joseph has left for us.

His childhood sandals made of palm bark and rough leather have long been out-grown. And now the many miles of rough travel are taking their toll on Joseph's tougher leather sandals. The condition of the soles of those sandals is comparable to his soul's transformation. The sandals show wear as if becoming wearier with every step.

So it is with a soul in transition. Transition in progress is the steps we take from the place we are at now to the place of completion. If one does not readily forgive injustices and quickly embrace God's refining grace, the burden can cause weariness to the soul.

The apostle Paul knew about and talks about this transition in Romans 12:1, 2. The Amplified Bible makes appeals us to move beyond the carnal thinking in this way;

"I appeal to you therefore, brethren, and beg of you in view of [all] the mercies of God, to make a decisive dedication of your bodies [presenting all your members and faculties] as a living sacrifice, holy (devoted, consecrated) and well pleasing to God, which is your reasonable (rational, intelligent) service and spiritual worship. Do not be conformed to this world (this age), [fashioned after and adapted to its external, superficial custom], but be transformed (changed) by the [entire] renewal of your mind [by its new ideals and its new attitude], so that you may prove [for yourselves] what is the good and acceptable and perfect will of God, even the thing which is good and acceptable and perfect [in His sight for you]."

ZEROING IN ON SPIRIT, SOUL AND BODY

In my teachings I often illustrate the concepts of our spirit, soul and body with white pieces of paper. The first is clean and white. *"The Spirit"* is written at the top. I inform the class that this is how God sees them after they have allowed the blood of Jesus to cleanse them from all unrighteousness. (I John 1:9)

The second paper represents the body with *"The Body"* written at the top. Below this I list things like exercise, optimal nutrition and healthy sleeping habits. I explain that we are responsible to care for our bodies because we are God's temples on earth. We must do our best to be healthy and attractive to carry out God's call in our lives.

We know God is preparing a new body for us in heaven, but He expects us to do our best to honor the gift of our body which He has given us. We must not—we may not live the sloppy habits of the world and expect to be our best for the kingdom of God.

My third part of the illustration is a packet of papers representing the soul. On the front I have written:

The way I view facts from my past

The way I react to data from the things that happened to me in my past

The way I allow the things of my past to affect my present

The way I allow the past to affect my plans for my future

I remind the class that our soul is our mind, our will and our emotions. Explaining that we are dealing with the issues of the unsurrendered soul I use a black marker and write descriptive words that deal with issues that have created our mindset and are manifested through our everyday lifestyle. I allow the class to help me come up with words like fear, failures, depression, discouragement, discontentment, verbal, mental, or sexual abuse, sexual sins, unbelief, unforgiveness, vices, ungodly habits, pride, neglect, injustices, ignorance, aggressiveness, manipulation, poverty mentality, suicidal attempts or desires, passivity, arrogance, revenge, jail record, arrests, revenge, cop-out mentality, murder, sickness or a sickness mentality.

Each person knows the components of his or her own soul better than anyone else and can make their own list of soulish issues.

UNSERSTANDING SOUL-JUNK

'Soul-junk' is a phrase I've coined for the issues of the mind, will and emotions that oppose the plans, purposes and process of God in our lives. Soul-junk is anything that does not conform to the will of God. These are areas of our mentality that disallow God's Word to be perfected through us. Many of us spend too much time thinking junkyard thoughts and never fulfill God's call in our lives.

There's a large junkyard not far from where we live. It is stacked, acre after acre, with old rusted car bodies of all makes and models. Rusted hoods lean against door-less vehicles. Shapes of the fancy 50's models can still be discerned through the weeds and brush, but it would be virtually impossible to rebuild most of those ancient cars that suffered wrecks, or just plain rusted out.

As I observe this junkyard I'm repulsed at someone holding on to their own past as well as the past of many other people, some who were killed in those distorted vehicles. Most of the skeletons of those autos have no wheels and sink into the marshes where they've been towed.

Why do I describe this junkyard?

It's because many of us have all sorts of "towed in" emotions that have nothing to do with God's plan for us. We try to use the junkyard of our past, the issues of the unsurrendered soul, as vehicles to convey us into our future. Imagine climbing into one of those junkyard models which have had the engine removed and trying to drive forward into your future. This concept, of course, is absurd. However, that is how many Christians still live their lives.

When we entered the kingdom of God we were given God's symbolic robe of righteousness that gives us access to every promise in Scripture. In order for us to fully appropriate these promises we must annihilate all areas of soul-junk.

GENERATIONAL CURSES

Deuteronomy 28:1-14 lists the blessings of God on His people if they will diligently listen to His commandments and obey them. The chapter then goes on to pronounce curses on those who won't listen to God's statutes and commandments. Verses 32 and 41 explain the curses that we pass down to our children if we don't listen to and obey the Word of God. Here is what God told Moses: *"Your sons and your daughters shall be given to another people, and your eyes shall look and fail with longing for them all day long...You shall beget sons and daughters, but they shall not be yours; for they shall go into captivity."*

Our wrong attitudes toward God, our selfish lifestyles, and our negative reactions to situations of life always pass down generational curses to our children. These things cause distractions and divert us from God's love.

Generational curses often steal into the core of our belief system unannounced. A child that receives rejection before its birth begins to form core values of life based on those negative emotions. Since abortion was legalized in our country in 1973, we have cruelly slaughtered well over fifty-three million of our babies. With this sanction of abortion in our society the value we place on our children is far below the value God places on them. This lack of respect for life opens doors to generational curses that are passed down to the most innocent and vulnerable.

When a parent thinks of their child as an inconvenience and talks down to him or her, that child will usually accumulate generational curses. Most of us, even Christians, have moved so far from the precepts of God's love, His righteousness and His Word that we are unaware of the dysfunctional lifestyles we live. One of the sayings I often heard as a child was "long-haired Dutch, don't know much," and other unkind words that led me to believe I was stupid.

The word-curses we speak to our children become generational curses. I cringe inside when I hear a mother say to her child, "You are making me angry!" (To become angry is by our own choice.) Or how about the parents that tell their child he/she never does anything right or will never amount to anything?

This is a sin! Ephesians 6:4 tells us to nurture our children. This is to rear them with tenderness, training them with counsel and disciplining them with the admonition of God's principles. To speak down to our children has the tendency to exasperate them and push them to a build-up of negative emotions of rebellion.

My generation has bought into a mentality that disregards God's Word as absolute truth. Rather than turning the tide back to God we have increasingly passed on generational curses to our children.

Where does suicide stem from? It stems from the lack of value a person places on his or her life. Why does the divorce rate continue to increase among Christians as fast as in the secular world? It's because we haven't aligned our mind, will, and emotions with God's promises to us. It is often because of our own selfish attitudes.

It is common for us to accept unhealthy and abnormal thinking without any idea that we're bound to mindsets and limitations caused by generational curses. Some generational curses are passed down in our physical DNA and affect our bodies and health. Why is it that we are required to fill out forms on the history of our family's health when we visit the doctor? It's because the doctor wants to know who has had cancer, heart problems, diabetes or other health deficiencies in our family tree. They tell us to be on guard for these health issues, as we'll probably have them too.

I am not advising anyone to be unwise by what I will say here, but I will challenge the mentality that we have bought into. Doctors have their place in the world, and so does pharmaceutical medication, so I am not telling you not to use these. One of the challenges we face here is how to use and not to abuse them.

Another challenge that strongly relates to the people of God is that we have adapted to the same lifestyle of eating and lack of exercise that the world has, and yet we expect God to somehow come and zap us with His healing strength. It is true that we must appropriate the virtues of Christ's cross, the power of God's Word for our healing and wholeness, but we must also be like Daniel was. In Daniel 1:8 we read that Daniel purposed in his heart not to defile himself with the king's meat, nor with the wine he drank.

Many of us have heard people say, "Diabetes runs in my dad's family, so I'll probably wind up with it too." What happens in this case is the person has more faith in his own DNA than in the healing words of God and in the powerful blood of Jesus. Where is our faith in God's Word? Consider the Psalmist's statement of faith in Psalm 118:17, *"I shall not die, but live, And declare the works of the LORD."* How will we respond to Scriptures like this?

Isn't it true that we just give in to the status quo and expect the same things that affected our parents or grandparents? The curses from past generations form our core values without giving us the understanding that we can overcome them. With all the new health care bills, changes of insurance policies and havoc in our government, we must move beyond our dependence on these agencies.

This is where the aspect of transition comes in. The caterpillar goes through a state of metamorphosis before it develops into a beautiful butterfly. I have never heard of a caterpillar that was afraid of going through that metamorphosis phase of life. We are of much more value than these beautiful creatures, so we must not parent our children from the standpoint of fear.

Parents who live in fear open doors to havoc and heartache in the lives of their children. Jesus came to bring us peace, but many of us don't know how to appropriate it. When we realize that Jesus gave us His peace and that Satan is the father of lies, we can choose to appropriate Christ's peace rather than to embrace the lies of Satan. It is vital for us to realize that the lies of Satan always and directly oppose the design God has planned for our lives. He desires for us to be like the three Hebrews who came out of the fire without having the smell of smoke on them. (Read the account in Daniel chapter three.)

With the understanding that generational curses are inherited issues that disrespect and annul God's precious promises to His children, take a few minutes to write out some of the generational curses in your own life that you're aware of.

_____

_____

_____

_____

_____

_____

_____

_____

_____

SELF CURSES

Some years ago I attended a ladies seminar on self-curses without understanding what the conference was about. This became one of my first eye-openers to issues of the unregenerated soul. I was surprised to find that much of the seminar's subject matter related to me in a direct way. As I listened to and worked through the spiritual exercises given, I understood what self-curses are and how to deal with them.

Self-curses are the lack of worth I place on myself, and these curses diabolically oppose what God has written about me in His Word. They are the mindsets I form that agree with the generational curses I've accumulated. They are the thought-patterns designed by self that disregard God's truth.

Isaiah 28:14, 15 gives us an understandable concept of self-curses. The prophet addresses *"...you scornful men,"* and then he tells what they have done. *"...you have said...'we have made lies our refuge, And under falsehood we have hidden ourselves.'"* Verse 20 tells us that these lies and falsehoods are too short for a bed to stretch out on, and too narrow for a cover to wrap up in (no robe of righteousness here). In reference to this scripture we realize that anything we adhere to that discredits the written Word is a piece of soul-junk. It actually falls under the category of lies and falsehoods as far as God is concerned.

That weekend I realized I'd made certain decisions concerning myself before I can remember making them. I had thought the screaming voice of "I hate myself" was the devil sitting on my shoulder screaming into my ear. I never understood why he didn't leave when I rebuked him. However, at this seminar I learned that at some point I had made the decision to hate myself and needed to repent of that decision. This self-curse was not a demon that needed to be rebuked, but it was an issue of my own making that I had to repent of. How could I receive God's generous love while I was choosing to hate myself?

Can you imagine how exciting that day was for me? It was a day of miraculous release where I gained understanding of and victory over that horrible oppression in my life. The things that had opposed me for years were overcome in a matter of minutes in the presence of God. Even though these thoughts still surface at times, I know what to do to overcome them. I repent of the sin of rejecting God's love and appropriate His love, forgiveness and grace.

A healthy attitude is to love ourselves with humility and respect, just as God loves us. This God-love is not pride, but rather a joyful submission to God's creation of the whole of us.

In my plain background, it was stressed that to keep children from becoming proud, they shouldn't be praised. I had often been teased in my childhood about being fat, and I assumed ugly went with it. That day these areas of self-rejections were dealt with. God met me at my altar, and through my tears I saw the beauty He had given me. This healing of the emotions brought me the release I needed to lose weight and accept what I didn't lose.

Another area that I still deal with is the "I can't" mentality. I grew up confessing this defeat on a daily basis. I spoke it as a six-year-old when I was expected to light our kerosene lamp and do chores that included milking our cows. How deeply that mentality of defeat had been engrained in my soul! Again I repented for having undermined the truth of Philippians 4:13, where Paul declares that he could do all things through Christ who strengthened him. My former defeat led me to conquest and victory.

Do you identify with any of these self-curses? Do you have any others you could add to the list of your faulty belief system?

I'll never love again.

This is going to kill me.

All men/women are jerks.

I'm a liar.

I'll never amount to anything.

I can't do anything right.

It doesn't matter anyway.

Whatever will be will be.

Nobody cares about me.

I'll never be loved.

Why should I care?

I'm just 'a nobody'.

I'm giving up!

I'm a lousy wife/cook/lover, etc.

I'll never tell.

I can't stand this any longer.

Nothing will ever change.

Add any other self-curses you face, and take the first steps of repentance. Deal with the issues that have enslaved you to your own soul. Accept the Father's love, His Son's atonement, and the comfort of the Holy Spirit to fill the areas you have just emptied of self-curses. You will be amazed at the difference this understanding will bring you.

STRONGHOLDS

After I had learned of self-curses that confirmed my generational curses, I was introduced to strongholds of my soul through the ministry of a precious sister, Liberty Savard. She teaches clearly on what strongholds are and how to loose them from us. God gave me a heart to learn many principles through her teaching and to make these principles my own personal message. Her two first books: *Shattering Your Strongholds* and *Breaking The Power* have been instrumental in helping me learn how to deal with my own unregenerated strongholds.

There are positive strongholds that the Bible speaks of. Scriptures portray God as a strong rock, a strong habitation or as having a strong arm. God and His spoken Word are the strongholds we adhere to, but we all have negative and destructive strongholds in our lives which we will address. We will learn to conquer them and climb to new understandings of God's love, mercy and grace.

You may have passed correction centers or institutions where tall woven wire fences are erected higher than anyone can reach. Strands of barbed wire secured above are intended to keep intruders out and prisoners in. This is how I see strongholds. Each one of us erects our own security fence of strongholds around the perimeter of all the generational and self-curses that we have collected.

My fence of strongholds was fortified with excuses, rationalization and justification of my unsurrendered soul. I had built my fence high enough that I thought nobody would ever trespass this area and really find out what was in the depth of my heart. Though I had erected these strongholds for my own protection they also kept me from receiving God's healing love.

My carnal reasoning reinforced my strongholds. My rationalization only strengthened my security fence with barbed wire of lies. My excuses would eventually defeat God's anointing as they banned His refining process from my life.

It's important for us to identify strongholds in our lives. Strongholds enslave us to the same reactions in adverse situations but without resolve of our conflicts. Recognizing strongholds will be our first step in dealing with this area of soul-junk.

Self and pride are strongholds that are first recognized as they flaunt themselves over the Lordship of Jesus Christ, His power to transform, and His healing touch. Selfishness is 'me-centered' and is displayed through self-indulgence, selfish ambitions, self-defense, self-pursuit, self-righteousness, selfish mindsets and selfish-reasoning.

It seems that pride was one of the first strongholds in Joseph's soul. It is one of the first strongholds God requires us to repent of and deal with. Jesus confirms this in Matthew 22:37 when he told the Pharisees, *"You shall love the LORD your God with all your heart, with all your soul, and with all your mind."* God wants to be first place in our life, our love, our mind and our emotions. As long as our own security fence of pride has not been uprooted it will bar the complete reversal of our self-curses. Haughtiness and legalism are aspects of pride.

Shyness is another offshoot of pride. As a young girl I was labeled as shy. I often hid behind that excuse for not speaking when I was spoken to or for not venturing out in new areas when I needed to. I remember the self-centeredness that revolved around that stronghold.

The concept that shyness is often introverted pride may seem strange to us, but can't we all relate to the mother who makes excuses for her child? The child has been given a sucker and the mother asks the child to say "thank you," but the child refuses to obey and hides behind his mother. The mother says, "I guess he's just feeling shy".

Dare I say (with all due respect to our children's various temperaments) that this child was not as shy as he or she was stubborn and focused on self? The mother was helping fortify her child's strongholds when she could have kindly and firmly ministered confidence to her child.

Shyness is an introversion that directs its attention on self. This is a link hidden in the middle of pride for no matter how you spell 'pride'—forward or backward—'I' is still in the middle of it. We readily make excuses for this introverted pride that opposes God's command in I Corinthians 10:31 *"...whatever you do, do all to the glory of God."* Glorifying God is God-focused, not me-focused. Shyness pleads for another's pity, but removing it leads to true humility.

Bitterness is another stronghold with deep roots. It links in with revenge, unforgiveness and self-vindication. These are justifications made by the will of man and defy God's access into the core of our hearts.

Fear is another stronghold that defeats God's gift of peace in our soul. When fear motivates us, is it any wonder that we limp toward our destiny or try to hide from peace-filled light? Allowing fear with its companions of anxiety and worry freezes us in our tracks and keeps us from the pursuit of Christ's destiny for us.

Fear weaves many links into this fence and labels them by different soulish identifications: fear of man, of failure, of the dark, of the past, of the future, of heat, of winter, of starvation, of crowds, and of being mobbed or looted. These are only a few of the fears that people excuse.

Jealousy and envy, two equally insidious strongholds, link in closely with murmuring, gossip, complaining and discontentment. They increase the restrictions and insecurities of the unregenerate soul.

We've already discussed some injustice done to Joseph and have seen how he could have felt like erecting strongholds as his defense system against further hurt. Joseph could have used excuses of the injustices done to him as grounds for fencing God out of his life, but I don't see him staying in bondage to any strongholds. He could have based strongholds on his fear of present circumstances or doubts about his future. If that had been the case, his strongholds could have disallowed God's divine intervention.

Because Joseph forgave, submitted and became subject to the situation of time and place, he was able to move ahead into God's perfect position at the exact time.

As each of us look into our own soulish reactions, reasoning and calculations we will find other areas of strongholds that we, as Joseph did, will have to deal with. By repenting of our pride and rebellion against God, we can begin to walk away from the strongholds of our unsurrendered soul and into our new and glorious liberty in Christ Jesus.

SOUL-TIES

When I think of soul-ties I think of them as posts set in place to hold up our security fence of strongholds. When our belief system is wrong, we build a fence of excuses and self-justifications around these beliefs. When our self-erected fence of strongholds no longer stands alone we will do our best to have others come into wrong agreements with us.

Many people rule their lives by forming soul-ties. We may use soul-ties to win arguments against those who point out our areas of needed change. When we've disallowed Biblical truth to rule our stubborn soul we often incorporate soul-ties, pulling others into agreement with our faulty belief system.

Soul-ties were evident in Joseph's life as he became entangled with his father's decision of picking favorites. Jacob willfully set Joseph over his brothers by making him the colorful coat. The fact that Joseph wore the coat proves that wrong agreements were being formed. God didn't want Joseph to become entangled with Jacob's soulish mentality. Though Joseph didn't understand it at the time, God used his adverse treatment to free him from those soul-ties.

This insight into the life of Joseph gives us clarity of how soul-ties can invade our lives. More often than not we acquire them quite innocently and without realizing what we've done. Here is an example of what I mean. If two of us are talking about a third party, hoping the other person will never know what we've said or prayed, we have come into wrong agreements with each other. It is important that we will not become sworn into secrecy.

There are other things that we must never become unified with. Anger, frustration, irritation, bitterness, fearfulness, worries, fretfulness, discontentment, unforgiveness and unscriptural demands are all things we must never pick up from those around us. Even if that person is our spouse, we must not come into agreement with ungodly characteristics of his/her soul. This doesn't mean that we don't love the other person, but we must decide not to agree with everything they say.

The angry person is embracing accusations that counter the plan of God. A frustrated person does not comprehend God's love for him or her. A fearful person opens doors into his own heart for turmoil and anxiety to enter. An irate person, contrary to God's plan, is unreasonable. Worry opposes God's promises of care, love and protection. Discontentment refuses God's supply. Bitterness comes into agreement with unforgiveness and diabolically opposes the Lordship of Jesus. The demanding person refuses to relinquish his or her rights to God.

This type of soul-junk hinders us from forming strong and lasting relationships with members of Christ's Body. If we come into wrong agreements about a third party we will have a guilty conscience when we meet that person and will usually start to imagine evil about him/her.

Caution must be taken not to come into wrong agreements because that can lead to witchcraft and sorcery. We need to discern the motive behind our friend's prayers before we come into full agreement with them. One person may pray for a big, new car and be praying in the will of God, while the next one, praying the same prayer, could be praying against God's will. One may desire to glorify God and further his/her ministry with the new car, while the other may be competing with her neighbors.

In John 17 Jesus prays that His followers may be one as He and His Father are one. Matthew 6:10 is another example of Christ's prayers: *"...Your kingdom come, Your will be done on earth as it is in Heaven."* Jesus never prayed a self-centered or personal-agenda type prayer. Praying against God's will hinders God's perfection in our lives.

There is a fine line between empathy and coming into wrong agreements with another person. God doesn't want divisions in His Body, but He wants us to be joined together that *"if one member suffers, all the members suffer with it; or if one member is honored all the members rejoice with it."* (I Corinthians 12: 26)

Dealing with soul-ties can be a touchy subject, therefore it is needful that one keep their own heart's motives pure and undefiled. This helps sharpen the discerning process and leads us to depend on God's unrelenting Word.

WHAT YOU HAVE LEARNED

We cannot move into the future by trying to resurrect our past.

Soul-junk is emotions that hinder God's plans, purposes and process in our lives.

Joseph was released from the grip of his father's wrong motives when he was sold as a slave.

The four areas of soulish-issues that we must all deal with are:

- Generational curses
- Self-curses
- Strongholds
- Soul-ties

AN EXERCISE TO PRACTICE

As we end this chapter, I want to encourage you to pray the following prayer as a pattern and a guide. As you use this for a model, you will become comfortable praying this type of prayer. You will find that you are stepping into areas of complete victory that you didn't know existed.

Dear Heavenly Father,

Thank you for sending us Jesus whose flesh was pierced, giving us access to every promise You have ever spoken to, by, or about us. Thank You for Jesus Christ, our port of entrance into Your Kingdom.

Lord, I have faced much turmoil in my life, but most of it has been of my own making because of the emotions that I have nurtured. Much of what I have believed has disagreed with Your plan for me. I confess every disloyal thought as sin, and I repent of each of them. Many of these thoughts are so deep I didn't know they were there, but now I release myself from the generational curses passed down on me. I loosen myself from self-curses by repenting of the things that I've allowed to deny Your grace. I pull down my strongholds, the things I have believed which disbelieve Your truth. I repent of the soul-ties, the wrong concepts and conversations that I've come into agreement with. I root out all soul-ties. You know each one of them. I choose to bring them all into submission to Your Word.

Lord, I choose to agree with everything You have said concerning me in Your written Word. I bow before You and acknowledge that <u>You are bigger than the defying circumstances of my life</u>. I choose to study Your Word and live my life according to its commands, which will bring me hope and purpose.

I thank You for the glorious liberty and spiritual authority I have as I walk in Your ways and Your truth. I thank You for the access to Your character and the authority of Your Word made available to me through Your Son, Jesus Christ.

Amen.

CHAPTER FIVE

On the Journey

~ Genesis 37:28 ~

We will gain assurance as we travel beyond the borders of the land that God had promised to give to Joseph's ancestors. Even though we find that life leads us into unexplored territory and through some hot, barren and desert lands, God's thoughts toward us are always for our own good. No set of circumstance can alter this truth! I am sure that neither Jacob nor Joseph could have gained comfort from this fact in their early separation, but eventually God's good thoughts were proven true.

LOOKING BEHIND THE SCENES

Do you remember that Reuben planned to rescue Joseph to deliver him to his father? By the time he, the oldest brother, has returned to the pit to rescue Joseph, this young brother has disappeared. It is not long, however, until he is told the whole story in full detail and shown the visual aid that will surely deceive their father.

Joseph's coat of many colors is in shreds, ripped in jagged tears. "Look at this Reuben!" the brothers exclaim excitedly. "Doesn't this look like some wild beast devoured Joseph? That should convince Father and clear us."

Reuben gasps in shock as he looks at the blood-splotched coat of his brother. Thinking they had killed Joseph, he opens his mouth in horror. His heartbeat races and a mixture of protests of their evil deeds clogs his mind. As he struggles to find his voice, the brothers laughingly explain that they actually hadn't killed Joseph but had sold him to a caravan of greedy Midianites.

"Here is your share of the money," Simeon says as he thrusts two pieces of silver into Reuben's hand. "We killed a lamb, dipped the coat in it's blood and stomped it into the dirt; and then we had lamb chops for supper."

"That should cover up for what we did and provide believable evidence!" The others cheer.

Reuben wants to do something, anything. He wants to run after the caravan and rescue Joseph. He wants to scream at his brothers, but he fears their cruelty. He hates what they've done but he holds his tongue and goes along with their plan.

The brothers know the possibility that their father will be out watching for Joseph's return, so they set off at a fast pace. Their plan is to beat the merchants to Hebron and distract their father so he will won't spot Joseph. Being young and tough, they over-drive their sheep and keep traveling throughout the night.

Breathlessly they rush up to the door and thrust the lying evidence into their father's hands. Jacob's brow creases with deep lines of concern as he quickly he scans the tribe in search of

Joseph. Panic strikes his heart, for it is evident that the brightly clad son is not among the brothers.

A wail of dismay pierces the air as Jacob rips his own cloak to show his intense agony. He falls to his knees and bows his head to the ground in desperation. His pleas for mercy and his questions hang heavily in the air, but the hard-hearted brothers have no pity on their father as he vows that he will go to his grave in mourning. Their hearts are hardened against Joseph but even harder toward their father.

The only relief that Jacob's cries bring is to the brothers. They are now relieved and confidence that Jacob will never see the caravan of Midianite merchants that is now passing through his back forty!

Their exploits have not failed. Their plot was believed. The lying evidence is mourned over, rehearsed daily and laid up as a regular reminder of their 'deceased' brother. Without even once being suspected, the brother's plan has been successful... or has it?

A COMPARISION

When the enemies of Jesus hung Him on the cross, watched Him die and pierced His side, they felt their task was completed. They gloated over the fact that their 'enemy' was dead without realizing Jesus has previously stated that he would lay down His life, that nobody could take it from Him. (See John 10:15-18)

God's kingdom is contrary to human thinking. In His kingdom, sickness leads to healing, trials lead to triumph, pressures lead to victory, darkness leads to light, and, finally, death leads to resurrection and eternal life.

From God's viewpoint things are seldom as they seem to us. Any opposing facts to God's Word or truth will eventually be subjected to that truth! Consider these aspects of God's kingdom to see how the facts lacked the full details of God's truth. Facts do not have the final say.

Three days of facts declared that Jesus was dead.

The grave reinforced that assumption.

Soldiers standing guard at the tomb secured the evidence.

The cross, freshly stained with Christ's blood, confirmed it.

The enemies of our Savior gloated over it.

BUT: In the end truth prevailed and Jesus arose from the grave! Remember this as we leave the brothers in their hardened conditions and Jacob in his relentless grief.

JOURNEYING WITH JOSEPH INTO EGYPT

Courtesy demands that we follow quietly and just close enough to Joseph to understand what he is experiencing.

Joseph, the young, handsome and strong teenager, finds himself trudging toward unknown territory after the most testing day of his life. What makes the trip so difficult isn't the walk itself, or the shackles with which he is bound, but it's the heaviness of being rejected by his brothers and facing a most unfortunate future of slavery.

The pain of the rejection turns into boiling hatred that first night out under the stars. He questions, "Now where is the God that my father told me about…the God that supposedly made all the big promises about my great-grandfather's seed being as the stars of the heaven?" The canopy of sparkling stars flung generously into the heavens seem to mock him.

Joseph sleeps very little this first night as he wrestles with his thoughts and angry feelings. Jacob had wrestled with an angel, but Joseph's thoughts are more tormenting than the angel had been. The angel had escaped by morning light, but Joseph's wrestling continues much farther into the journey.

Hatred gives way to momentary hope as Joseph passes along his father's back acreage. Listen as Joseph yells at the top of his voice, "Father, Father, do you hear me? I'm right here going past your place," but there's no answer.

Joseph realizes that his father wouldn't recognize him without his coat of many colors. Now he is stripped bare of his identity, shackled, and not recognized as the beloved son. Nobody knows that he really is somebody! Tears most assuredly wash his face dozens of times as he wearily plods toward Egypt.

I WANTED TO JOIN JOSEPH'S PITY PARTY

Knowing the nature of humanity, it is only likely that Joseph had to deal with self-pity as he trudged the 300 long miles into Egypt. Here he was, trudging toward an unknown destination against his will. Though he had human flaws and soulish issues to deal with, the offense could hardly have been great enough to merit this type of injustice.

Knowing what taking a journey against one's will was like, I cried for Joseph when I started this study. Some years ago, when my husband and I moved from San Antonio to Wisconsin, I left emotional skid marks from my heels of reluctance on the long miles of Interstate 35. I, the mother of three beautiful daughters, had often found my identity through them. Now they were all left behind, even my sixteen-year-old! I also left behind work I loved, my circle of friends, and a glowing halo of being a missionary to the Philippines.

When I arrived in northwest Wisconsin, nobody knew me and I didn't know a thing about my new and unsolicited job. Having moved from a hot climate in the middle of August, the cool and damp Wisconsin autumn weather seemed as desolate as my heart and the coming of winter with its bitter cold only emphasized the effect.

Needless to say, I was having the ultimate and loneliest pity party all by myself! I poured myself lavish cups of blame and locked myself away from God's grace. I replayed my "poor me" mentality and gave in to crying fits. I furnished my pity party with a whole assortment of 'vivid videos of recall' to review all the injustices of my past.

It took me years to realize the problem was mine and that I needed to face the issues of my own unforgiving soul. Finally I allowed God to erase my skid marks on Interstate 35, and today I can say, "God brought me to this place for a purpose." Do I know what that purpose is? I may see a small part of it, but I am still a person in progress. I am holding onto Joseph's examples for my own transformation.

The 'poor-Joseph' mentality, if sincerely examined, could translate into a 'poor-me' mentality. We may find ourselves plodding into our own Egypt against our will and never let go of our emotional coat of many colors. In this way we are hindering ourselves from moving beyond areas of our own soul-junk. God still had glory and purpose awaiting Joseph as he moved away from the pain of his past. We too can journey through God's process of refinement with dignity and purpose.

VICTORY BEGINS WITH OUR THOUGHT LIFE

Since Joseph's journey into Egypt is 300 miles long and leads through some forsaken and dangerous territory, he has a lot of time to think. After the initial anger and shock of the situation wears off, Joseph begins to take charge of his thought-life. By now he realizes he is not getting out of his shackles and running back home to his father! Joseph further recognizes the only hope he has for survival is to remember the faith he embraced.

Will this faith work now… in these circumstances?

Bitterness, blame, revenge and anger all plead for preeminence in Joseph's emotions. He has to make a series of hard choices about what to allow in his thought life. Will he replay the injustices done to him so many times that they will drown out forgiveness, love, mercy and restoration? His emotions run high, and his hurt cuts deeply into the core of his being.

Can he still believe that he is in line for Abraham's seven-fold blessing found in Genesis 12? Can he even remember the blessing in these blowing desert sands?

He shakes himself, forcing his mind to focus. *"I will make you a great nation."* That is the first one. Now he has six more to go. One by one they come into his mind. *"I will bless you."* "I wonder if that promise applies to me," I can hear him whisper under his breath.

"I will make your name great… you shall be a blessing."

"Well, God, how do You plan to do that? With the special favor my father bestowed on me I was well on my way to having a great name. Now I don't even have a coat to sleep in at night."

Joseph pulls his thoughts back into alignment with God's promises as he continues to recount the next promise. *"You will be a blessing."*

Now his heart's cry turns into a prayer, "Lord, could You really make me a blessing to anyone? Do I dare hope that the dreams will still be fulfilled?"

Then the fifth part of the covenant comes to him as if in answer to his questions. *"I will bless those who bless you."*

Joseph's steps are feeling lighter as he rehearses the last two promises. *"I will curse them that curse you, in you will all the families of the earth be blessed."*

"Lord, could that be me?" New hope is dawning on his horizon.

WHAT DO WE DO?

The "what do you do now?" questions still remain for us to answer.

What do you do when you're stripped of your identity?

What do you do when you're sold into slavery, serving people you don't know or like?

What do you do when nobody knows you are somebody?

What do you do when you've been visited by God and given a mandate, but suddenly your plans are destroyed, and you're searching for your purpose in life?

What do you do when you've been lied about and cut off from family, friends and familiarity?

What do you do when you're being moved to unfamiliar surroundings against your will?

What do you do when the hot sands sting your bare body and the sun keeps beating down on you?

What do you do when the chains you are bound with cut into your biceps and external pain is emphasized by additional internal pain?

What do you do when nobody seems to understand what you are saying?

What do you do when you find yourself in Egypt, which symbolizes a life of the flesh?

The question is: what are we to do when we find ourselves in such a predicament? What can, should, or must we do?

ACTION STEPS FOR AN OVERCOMING LIFESTYLE

When we cooperate with God's written word we steadily step beyond our own limitations. My intent here is to bring us doable steps of agreement with God and His plan for us.

1. Walk by faith, not by sight

II Corinthians 5:7 says, *"For we walk by faith, not by sight."*

Into whatever circumstance this journey of life may bring us, we keep right on marching...walking by faith! We keep right on marching and let the sun keep on bearing down on us. It will tan us after it burns us, and then sweet will be our healing! We keep right on marching though we wanted to get off at Hebron to expose those who oppressed us. We keep right on marching and remember our visitations from God and the promises He has given.

Joseph's journey was one of faith, as he had no power over his circumstances or future. It seemed that he had become unimportant and was heading into an unplanned destination. Though the journey was defined with purpose and promise in the heart of God, it was undefined in Joseph's thinking. It had come so unexpectedly and uninvited that it could have left Joseph's emotions on an unstoppable roller-coaster!

However, as he recalled the seven-fold covenant of God to his great-grandfather Abraham he found his survival plan. Romans 10:17 tells us that faith comes by hearing God's word. God's word builds faith in His children, giving us strength to keep marching in our own desert sands of injustice. Joseph didn't have all the precious promises written out like we do and yet he kept developing his faith.

2. Refuse to hold on to facts rather than God's word

Facts are easier for us to believe than God's truth because they involve our senses (taste, touch, smell, sight and hearing), whereas God's word is activated by faith.

Ephesians 4:23, 24 commands, *"and be renewed in the spirit of your mind, and put on the new man which was created according to God, in true righteousness and holiness."*

Romans 12:2 directly confirms our need to release facts and embrace God's Word. *"And do not be conformed to this world, but be transformed by the renewing of your mind, that you may prove what is that good and acceptable and perfect will of God."*

The process of renewing our mind to embrace God's word isn't easy, but its outcome is eternal!

3. Persevere past the turmoil of your life

When our girls were young, our three-year-old was often waking up with nightmares. She told us Jesus was by her bed but Satan came and told Him to go away. This happened several nights in a row until we gave the little tyke II Timothy 1:7 to memorize: *"For God has not given us a spirit of fear, but of power and of love and of a sound mind."*

Before the day was over she had memorized it, so we instructed her to say it if she had bad dreams again. That night we again heard her cry of terror, but as we approached her room we heard her soft voice declaring, "God has not giben me a pirit of fear, but of pow'r un lob and a sound mind." She fell asleep immediately upon her confession.

Paul, the apostle who had faced one crisis after another, knew that the spirit of fear did not come from God. The tests of his faith had taught him that God gives each of us power, love and a sound mind. In using Strong's number system #4994 and 4995, we find that a sound mind is a correct or self-disciplined mind.[1] Its thought patterns are organized by sobriety and sound judgment.

Screaming emergencies, fearful evidences, and dreadful happenings demand that we become scared, but faith looks to God and proclaims, *"...for I know whom I have believed and am persuaded that He is able to keep what I have committed to Him until that Day."* (II Timothy 1:12) The word "keep" implies the

Lord setting Himself apart to watch over that very thing we have entrusted to Him. He will not sleep nor be distracted from taking care of the said situation once it's been placed into His keeping.

As our three-year-old daughter did, so you and I can also persevere beyond the turmoil of our lives.

4. We allow God to be our avenger

No matter how bad we want to get revenge and retaliate, we let God be our righteous judge and our avenger. He said, *"Vengeance is Mine, I will repay;"* (Romans 12:19). We bring to mind the horrible sufferings of Christ Jesus who, *"though He was a Son, yet He learned obedience by the things which He suffered."* (Hebrews 5:8)

As we trust in God's vindication, we discover how to give thanks even though we are weeping and let God turn our sorrows into joy. We obtain grace to embrace the fire through which we are passing, and refuse to let go of our redemption's song. We refuse to forget Romans 12:2 where Paul commands us to be transformed by renewing our mind, and we allow old things to pass away according to II Corinthians 5:17.

With freedom and direction we keep right on marching for as long as our 300-mile journey will take us.

WHAT YOU HAVE GAINED SO FAR ON THE JOURNEY

Reuben's plan to rescue Joseph had failed, as our own plans often do.

Jacob vowed to die in mourning for his son, an example of self-pity at it's worst.

Jacob looked at lying evidences the same way that Christ's crucifixion was viewed by those present.

Victory begins with our thought life.

Mile by mile and day by day Joseph gained understanding of how God works in our lives.

We must walk by faith and not by sight.

We need to refuse to hold onto facts rather than God's Word.

We are given power to persevere past the turmoil of our lives.

We do well to allow God to be our avenger.

AN EXERCISE TO PRACTICE

In the last chapter we addressed four areas of soulish entanglements, and now we have seen how Joseph is allowing his unjust treatment to grow him into an overcomer. In this chapter we are emphasizing four action steps to an overcoming lifestyle. To help you own these concepts, copy these four points and memorize the Scriptures that are here associated with each one. You can enlarge your reference base by adding your own Scriptures to these powerful seeds for growing your faith.

1. I will live by faith and not by sight

II Corinthians 5:7 says, *"For we walk by faith, not by sight."*

2. I will refuse to hold onto facts rather than God's Word

Ephesians 4:23, 24 *"and be renewed in the spirit of your mind, and put on the new man which was created according to God, in true righteousness and holiness."*

3. I will persevere past the turmoil of my life

II Timothy 1:7 *"For God has not given us a spirit of fear, but of power and of love and of a sound mind."*

4. I will allow God to be my avenger

"Though He was a Son, yet He learned obedience by the things which He suffered." (Hebrews 5:8)

Joseph's Journey Ends

~ Philippians 4:6-9 ~

*A*s Joseph's journey is ending we see that the process of his refinement is just beginning. Though the blowing sands of the desert have toughened his skin, his heart is being softened. By releasing Joseph from his prison of ancient history portraying him one of God's children who walks among us today, we can see how he's doing as this undesirable adventure progresses.

The merchants point to a speck on the distant horizon and Joseph senses that this portion of his journey is about to end. As the cargo is unloaded, Joseph is led to a group of other youth from various parts of the world. They are all still bound with shackles as night again finds them sleeping out under the stars with a night guard keeping vigilance over them.

What is he to expect in this strange land? How will he ever learn to communicate in this foreign language? Where will he be by tomorrow night? Sleeplessness ensues as his questions grow and intensify. Finally when he dozes off under the canopy of stars—the stars that now remind him of the Abrahamic covenant—he becomes aware of another presence. At first the vision is dim, but then he sees that Jesus, who would be revealed to this world at a future date, has been marching with him throughout his journey into Egypt.

Joseph hears the compassionate voice of Christ speak directly to him from the prophecy of Isaiah 53: *"I too was despised and rejected of man. I was a man of sorrows, and grief was My companion and acquaintance. I have borne your griefs and sorrows for you. I was wounded for the times you transgressed My commandments and heedlessly plundered My law. The bruising I bore in My body was to purge you from your iniquities. I took the chastisement in My own body so that you would have access to My peace."*

"Because I am the righteous servant, I justify you and many more along with you. I am now making intercession for you so that you will avail yourself to all the blessings I have made possible for you."

JOSEPH AGREES WITH GOD'S PROMISES

Joseph's eyes flash open as he realizes God was with him throughout this journey. The word of God's truth had been received in the heart of this young overcomer. As he ponders his visitation, his mind flashes back to Hebron and he remembers his God-given dreams.

Joseph chooses to agree with what God promised him in Jeremiah 29:11. This portion of Scripture gives us an awesome reflection on God's thoughts. *"For I know the thoughts that I think* toward you," says the LORD, "thoughts of peace and not of evil, to give you a future and a hope." God's thoughts are only thoughts of peace to give us a secured end. To understand this is to bring our minds into submission to His Word. As Joseph remembers the precious promise God has given him, he is engulfed with a sweet peace in a distant and strange land.

Transformation takes place when we agree with the things God says, for His words are all precious, true and eternal. Why agree with anything less?

Psalm 40:5 is further confirmation to God's good intent for His children. *"Many, O LORD my God, are Your wonderful works which You have done; and Your thoughts toward us cannot be recounted to You in order; if I would declare and speak of them, they are more than can be numbered."*

Isaiah 55:9 declares, *"For as the heavens are higher than the earth, so are My ways higher than your ways, and My thoughts than your thoughts."*

We must focus on God's Word and agree with Isaiah 26:3, *"You will keep him in perfect peace, whose mind is stayed on You, because he trusts in You."* The needful thing to do in time of despair is to refocus on the times of our refreshing, looking back on what we've been taught, and recounting our Godly heritage.

HE ESTABLISHES A NEW IDENTITY

As our young hero has ended his journey through the barren miles of desert he has come to the place that he realizes that he will never again wear his colorful coat that his father had made and given to him. He will have to come up with a new identification of who he is. The choices he make will establish his future and as we keep stride with him, we will see him make the kind of choices that give him an outstanding identification.

Our robe of many colors can be any favor of God or man, wrongfully received or reacted to. It could also be wrong agreements we've established. When this old identification is stripped from us, no matter how cruelly, we must embrace our new identity…one that's rooted by grace, in faith. We see ourselves through Calvary's love and not through the painful things that have befallen us.

We make the issues of our heart be the things of importance and forget about our coat of many colors. We reestablish our identification by wrapping ourselves in God's robe of righteousness. We make the adjustments of mind, will and emotion that are needed to move from our self-righteousness to the security of God's robe of righteousness.

We allow the journey to prepare us for what lies ahead of us by letting go of the past with all its injustices, pain and broken dreams. As we keep on marching, we establish our present and anticipate our future.

MEMORIZE SCRIPTURES

Have you tried to memorize scriptures? Most of us think it's impossible. We can memorize TV commercials, cheers for our ball team, and tainted jokes, but don't expect us to memorize scripture. Why is this?

My own experience has taught me that when I have a difficult time memorizing scripture it's either because I do not understand what the portion means, or it's because I do not want the words to transform me. The reality is, I am not ready to embrace something in the verse to the degree of being changed. I am too lazy to deal with it, so I allow the opportunity of the moment to by-pass me while I allow my mind to think about things of lesser value.

Now is the time to take back wrong thought-pattern-territory. Deuteronomy 6:6-9 tells us how to do this:

> *"...these words which I command you today shall be in your heart. You shall teach them diligently to your children, and shall talk of them when you sit in your house, when you walk by the way, when you lie down, and when you rise up. You shall bind them as a sign on your hand, and they shall be as frontlets between your eyes. You shall write them on your doorposts of your house and on your gates."*

Following these simple guidelines for our daily life will automatically provide opportunity for Scripture memorization.

Most of our homes are not geared to talk of God's ways. A few of us may try shouting them at our children above the din of self-entertainment. We don't have much time to take walks with our children, but what if we turned down the radio and recited Scriptures on our way to ballgames or ballet? With what do we tuck our children into bed or awake them? I suggest using Scriptures and songs of God's love.

In II Timothy 2:15 Paul commands, *"Be diligent to present yourself approved to God, a worker who does not need to be ashamed, rightly dividing the word of truth."* The only way we can handle God's Word without timidity or hesitation is to be thoroughly saturated with it. We need to dig into its truths, concepts and depths. This will help our memorization process and its application to the weak areas in our lives. These Godly habits will automatically counter wrong feelings.

DELIGHTING IN GOD

As we read the Psalms we find that David experienced highs and lows in the range of emotions. He, like Joseph, knew what unjust treatment was, and yet he penned the beautiful words of Psalm 37:1-5. These are some of my favorite verses in the book of Psalms.

"Do not fret because of evildoers, Nor be envious of the workers of iniquity." (Don't sip from your 'almost-empty cup' of self-pity as you rehash the injustices done to you.)

"For they shall soon be cut down like the grass, and wither as the green herb." (God will take care of your enemies.)

"Trust in the LORD, and do good; dwell in the land, and feed on His faithfulness." (Trust is positive and leads confidently to doing good.)

"Delight yourself also in the LORD, and He shall give you the desires of your heart." (Sporting ourselves in God's luxurious grace will bring us our heart's desires.)

"Commit your way to the LORD, trust also in Him, and He shall bring it to pass." (Commitment and trust lead us to our rainbow's end…the fulfillment of our dreams.)

Often we've lost touch with our inner desires and have no idea what makes us happy. The key is to pursue the praises of God for He knows just how to press our 'happy button' and fulfill our heart's desires. We won't even know what has happened, but we will suddenly realize that the emptiness inside us is filled and the deep longing is gone. God has granted us our desires!

THE 'I HAVES' I POSSESS

The following scriptural concepts will help you develop a mindset of faith. Call this your list of 'I HAVES', and make this your confession. "I have…"

- 📖 Salvation: Acts 16:31 *"…Believe on the Lord Jesus Christ, and you will be saved…"*

- 📖 Healing: I Peter 2:24 *"…by whose stripes you were healed."*

- 📖 Health: Isaiah 33:24 *"And the inhabitant shall not say, 'I am sick;'"*

- 📖 Wisdom: James 1:5 *"If any of you lacks wisdom, let him ask of God, who gives to all liberally and without reproach. And it will be given to him."*

- 📖 Strength: Isaiah 40:29 *"…to those who have no might He increases strength."*

- 📖 Boldness: Proverbs 28:1 *"…the righteous are bold as a lion."*

- 📖 Financial Supply: Philippians 4:19 *"And my God shall supply all your need according to His riches in glory by Christ Jesus."*

- 📖 Power: Acts 1:8 *"…you shall receive power when the Holy Spirit is come upon you…"*

- 📖 Peace: John 14:27: *"…My peace I give to you…"*

📖 Forgiveness: Ephesians 1:7 *"In Him we have redemption through his blood, the forgiveness of sins..."*

📖 The Mind of Christ: I Corinthians 2:16: *"...we have the mind of Christ."*

📖 Righteousness: II Corinthians 5:21 *"For He made Him who knew no sin to be sin for us, that we might become the righteousness of God in Him."*

📖 Sanctification and Redemption: I Corinthians 1:30 *"But of Him you are in Christ Jesus, who became for us... sanctification and redemption."*

📖 Ability to Witness: Acts 1:8b *"...you shall be witnesses to Me..."*

📖 Fruitfulness: John 15:5 *"...He who abides in Me, and I in him, bears much fruit;"*

EIGHT WAYS TO LEGALIZE YOUR THOUGHTS

"I thought you had a right to think anything you want to think," I can hear someone object. "What are you saying when you say you want to legalize my thoughts?"

The authorized-by-God, Kingdom-of-God, legal thought patterns are clearly spelled out in Philippians 4:8. These eight legalized-by-God thought types are:

True things
Noble things
Just things

Pure things
Lovely things
Things of good report
Virtuous things
Praiseworthy things

Somehow and somewhere during Joseph's journey and life of testing, he recognized the God-given mandate to meditate on these thought types. He appropriated them for his own as he moved ahead in life.

WHAT YOU HAVE LEARNED FROM THIS JOURNEY

In this chapter we have learned that:

To cooperate with God is your most direct thoroughfare to the fulfillment of your destiny.

We must agree with what God says about us.

We need to memorize Scriptures that counter wrong feelings.

We must delight ourselves in God at all times.

We must establish our new identity in Christ.

There are eight legal, God-authorized thought types that we should practice.

LET'S CHECK OUR OWN PROGRESS

By answering the following "yes" and "no" questions, we can easily check our own progress in our spiritual growth.

Are the emotional landmarks I'm passing familiar?

Are the faces of my abusers still clearly defined in my mind?

Am I still recalling the accusations of my childhood?

Am I still paralyzed (to the point of being unable to minister healing to others) by the death of my spouse, a child or loved one of a decade ago?

Am I still having nightmares because of an unpleasant experience in my past?

Am I blaming God or someone else for a predicament I am in?

Am I thinking that suicide may be my easiest route of escape?

Do I continuously react to adverse situations in the same way?

Do I find that my past hurts are foretelling my future?

Are the questions I have asked for years unanswered still?

Do I feel hopeless, like nothing will ever change?

Am I coming upon burial grounds with markers that read any of the following?

- Here lies integrity.

- Here lies forgiveness.

- Here lies faithfulness.

- Here lies the fear of God.

- Here lies wisdom.

- Here lies fervency.

- Here lies honesty.

- Here lies the love of truth.

- Here lies _____.

If you answered "yes" to any of these questions, you need to go back to the section of the 'I haves' in this chapter.

To see how to deal with the areas of the soul that remain unresponsive to God's absolute truth, we need to search our own hearts to see what causes the emotional dysfunction of our journey into Godliness. God doesn't want us spinning our emotional wheels in the doubt of rationalization. He doesn't want us to pass the same signposts of fleshly reactions or keep limping along on our broken emotional crutches.

God wants us to grasp the mindset and thought-patterns that He has intended for us to have. Some of us have never heard of the power of a transformed mind. He longs for us to resurrect all the attributes of Godliness that we have trampled underfoot or buried along the way. God wants our unhealed "self" to be whole in Him.

Write out here which soulish areas you still need to work at overcoming.

_____

_____

_____

_____

_____

Now write out what you will allow yourself to think about.
Which of the eight virtues will you apply to yourself?

_____

_____

_____

_____

_____

_____

_____

_____

_____

_____

_____

_____

_____

The Slave's Garment

~ Genesis 39:1-20 ~

J oseph has been sold to Potiphar, the captain of Pharaoh's guard. He is now in his slave's quarters after his first grueling day of duty to this high ranking officer. Come; let us listen in on this new slave's prayer.

"Not the garment of a slave, Lord! I didn't ask for this identification! I know I felt bare and naked without any identity, but not this, Lord! How can I lift my head without shame and despair? Why have You chosen this garment for me? What have I done to deserve such degrading shame?"

We can plainly see the tears stream down Joseph's cheeks as he cries out in agony. The wounding on his journey has been sore, but now the stripes cut deeper into his heart.

He now begins to understand the cries that must have been in his great-grandfather Abraham's heart when he was called to sacrifice his promised son. Oh how deep the pain—how it must have cut! Could there not have been an easier way? He cries out in his Hebrew tongue, "Is this the way it must be for me? Where is the ram that You provided for Abraham? What is my route of escape?"

His pleas are anguished as he cries long into the night. Has God disappeared into the darkness? He searches his own soul, thumbs through the pages of his mind, rumbles through the debris of his emotions, and finally subdues his will to the God of his forefathers, making God's will his own.

ADJUSTMENTS MUST BE MADE

As Joseph awakens early the next day, he faces the challenge of wearing the scant garment that identifies him as one of Potiphar's slaves. He feels naked and exposed as he steps from the tiny space in the slave's quarters.

Unlike the Hebrew's modest clothing, Joseph has been given the skirt-like garment of the Egyptians. It fastens around his waist and hangs down toward his knees. Thus his tanned shoulders are exposed and his chest is bare as he executes the office of a slave. His biceps ripple with appealing strength as he carries heavy water pots and grinds corn at the mill.

How Joseph's emotions must reel! First he was the chosen, favored, set-apart son who freely spoke his mind, and now he faces the challenge of having a limited vocabulary. He sets out to conquer and learns quickly.

Everyone he meets is a stranger, from the high ranking Potiphar, to the slaves that share his quarters. Joseph sets out to please and serve his master. God has anointed him for the difficult situation he was in. He sets out to find his bearings, the boundaries of the plantation, the routine of executing daily chores and the oversight of all that is required to equip the home front.

Potiphar's house is Joseph's first exposure to such grandeur. His challenge of serving in an acceptable way leads to his heartfelt tears at night. As he cries to God for help, God enables him to find his natural bent, that of serving. He conquers the strangeness and makes it his familiar domain.

Because of his faith in God, Joseph is commissioned to see to the wellbeing of all that Potiphar owns. He is given the oversight and entrustment of his crops, livestock and household.

THE IMPORTANCE OF THE REFINER'S FIRE

In every phase of our Christian walk there will be a time of refinement. My mother left us a godly example of facing one phase of refinement after another; that of going hungry, being excommunicated, verbal abuse, divorce, the loss of a child, and the list goes on and on. However, she always sang her song and moved through the refining process in victory. Her refinement is now complete as she is in the presence of the one she loves the most… the Lord Jesus Christ.

The first time I learned anything about this refining fire came through a God-given dream in my adolescent years. God showed me a piece of royal blue fabric with "Matthew 3:11" embroidered on it in red thread. I memorized the words which John the Baptist spoke to the Sadducees and Pharisees.

> *I indeed baptize you with water unto repentance: but he that cometh after me is mightier than I, whose shoes I am not worthy to bear: he shall baptize you with the Holy Ghost, and with fire. (KJV)*

At that point I didn't even understand God's plan of salvation for me, let alone know what the baptism of the Holy Ghost or the baptism of fire was. Now I know that God's plan for us is to be empowered by His Holy Spirit and refined by His fire. This baptism of fire will not destroy anything of importance to God. Our job is to embrace His cleansing process.

Hebrews 12:1-6 admonishes us not to become weary in our times of testing.

Therefore we also, since we are surrounded by so great a cloud of witnesses, let us lay aside every weight, and the sin which so easily ensnares us, and let us run with endurance the race that is set before us, looking unto Jesus, the author and finisher of our faith, who for the joy that was set before Him endured the cross, despising the shame, and has sat down at the right hand of the throne of God.

For consider Him who endured such hostility from sinners against Himself, lest you become weary and discouraged in your souls. You have not yet resisted to bloodshed, striving against sin. And you have forgotten the exhortation which speaks to you as to sons: "My son, do not despise the chastening of the LORD, Nor be discouraged when you are rebuked by Him; For whom the LORD loves He chastens, and scourges every son whom He receives."

I have found it interesting to see how the Psalmist associates God's love and his trials as one. As we compare Psalm 11:5 with Psalm 146:8 we see that God both tests and loves the righteous.

The love that God has for His children cannot be separated from the tests He puts us through. The King James Version of the Bible says, *"The Lord trieth the righteous."* This means that God investigates and examines us to prove us and find us true.

I Peter 1:7 assures us that the Refiner's fire, the testing of our faith, is more precious than perishable gold. Peter further explains that we should not consider our times of testing a strange thing, but we should embrace those tests through true worship of God.

INTEGRITY PLAYS ITS ROLE

As we revisit Joseph, we see that through all the changes and roller-coaster emotions, he holds onto his integrity and asserts himself in learning independently. The roots of his faith change him from being a spoiled little kid to being a man of quality production. Though he is in a land of a different language, he becomes an effective communicator.

Joseph is now far removed from the quiet hillside where his sheep had grazed contently and the spring air had blown softly through his hair! Now there are no cool streams and noontime meditation. Yet amid this drastic change of pace, Joseph manages his time and the details he is given in an orderly manner.

He utilizes the hours of night and early morning to cultivate his faith and exercise himself as a creative thinker. He finds amazing strength from the inception of his deeply founded faith. God's wisdom heightens his natural understanding and gives him an amazing ability to execute the most demanding tasks.

The grace and favor on his life soon bring him to the place of distinction as an outstanding business manager. He has climbed the ladder, one rung at a time, until he is above his fellow slaves and where his slave's garment is no longer his only identification.

Joseph's master has his eyes on him as he recognizes Joseph's confidence and leadership ability. This is why Potiphar has promptly promoted him to the position of top slave. He knows he can leave the house with the confidence that Joseph will execute the details of his charge. Potiphar has found a bargain in this quick-learning, energetic and capable slave!

JOSEPH IN THE WORKPLACE

It is only possible to touch the tip of the iceberg here when it comes to Joseph's work ethics. Joseph's work habits are ingrained in him as moral obligations and duty. His great-grandfather, Abraham, had been greatly blessed of God because he was diligent about his business. Abraham passed this blessing of hard work on to his son Isaac. Isaac is known for the wells he dug and for reaping a hundred-fold harvest in the year of famine (see Genesis 26:12).

We know that Isaac's son Jacob also taught his sons at a young age to tend his cattle and be responsible. Joseph inherited the concept of availing himself to every opportunity that was afforded to him. He realized that a lesson taught through his mistakes is never a meaningless lesson unless he fails to learn the lesson that mistake was to teach him.

Joseph's opportunity came to him wearing a disguise, that of being a slave. This too is how God often presents us with opportunity, many of which are lost because we do not discern God's unending love for us.

Joseph brakes out of the stigma of being a mere slave. He doesn't only survive on the meager crumbs of a slave's portion, but he actually prospers in this lowly workplace. He pushes forward with the work skills he's learned. He becomes mighty in his methods of cooperation and willing in the execution of his duties. In doing so he not only makes Potiphar prosper, but he also prospers...expediting honored responsibility.

IT'S TIME TO MEET MRS. POTIPHAR

No, we won't be staring at a movie screen as we see this sensual story unfold. This is the true story of our handsomely tanned hero and the seducing Mrs. Potiphar. Unlike most of today's movies, this man will make some deliberate and right choices.

It isn't long until Mrs. Potiphar also takes note of Joseph. At first Joseph innocently dodges her, but she will not be ignored! Day by day she lays wait for him, trying to corner him into being alone with her in the house.

When Joseph can no longer ignore and dodge her, he appeals to her, "I've been entrusted by your husband with all that's here in his house, except for you. You are his wife. How could I sin so against him and God?"

Potiphar's wife is not used to being denied and obviously gets whatever she wants without considering another's cost. She depicts everything that our soul and flesh demand of us. She is very graphically described in Proverbs 7 as the strange woman and the crafty harlot.

The definition for the strange woman in Strong's #2114 is, "to turn aside, to be a foreigner, profane and to commit adultery[1]."

She looks for the young and foolish that she longs to lure into her web of immorality. She considers every man that she makes a pass at as someone who is simple, foolish, void of understanding, and willing to be led astray. In this way she is degrading, humiliating and cheapening him as a person.

She lays wait in shadows and darkness for any man that she might trap. She wears the disguise of a harlot, flinging her sensuality in brazen tones and allurement. The tones of her voice are low and enchanting as she persuades the simple into her lovely bedroom and lavishly decked bed. She promises her catch that they will not be disturbed and that he can rest in the afterglow of their affair. Her false promises are deliberate lies that she sets to trap him.

Potiphar's wife, young and lovely, is a cheap, flaunting deceiver. She plans a death trap for Joseph, knowing that the usual punishment for this type of sin is the execution of its subjects. She is not used to encountering a Joseph who has convictions and this makes her want him even more. Her sensual pursuit of this handsome young Hebrew allows Satan to take advantage of her idle mind. She schemes and plots to get her way with Joseph.

In her craftiness she sends all the other servants from the house when she knows it is time for Joseph to come and do his chores in the halls of her palace. She had heard his denial of her request, but she continues to impose her corrupt intentions upon him.

As Joseph ascends the lavish stairs into the palace he is surprised to find the usual bustle is not awaiting him in the halls. As he busies himself at the far end of the palace, he ponders the steps he had taken to acquire this position. He has served willingly and God has poured into him wisdom beyond his years. Joseph hums an old Hebrew tune from his childhood as he goes from room to room performing his duties.

"How strange it is that there's nobody else in the house this morning," Joseph says to himself. Just then he hears light footsteps in the hall and is jolted back to reality.

"Oh Joseph, there you are! I've been waiting all morning for you to come and make up my bed," Mrs. Potiphar lies, "please come immediately so I can think about other things."

On his way down to Mrs. Potiphar's room Joseph again vows that he will not fall prey to her sensual allurements. He realizes that he needs to be ready to make a fast escape if the situation demands it.

No sooner are they inside the room than she deftly removes her own robe and grabs hold of his slave garment. Joseph, the stronger, leaves his garment in her hand and flees for the sake of moral purity.

Potiphar's wife, the beauty queen, the pampered lady, the seducing soul, further lowers herself by lying to her husband. This cover-up of her evil is her way of getting an innocent person killed or imprisoned. Her plot works...or does it?

THE IMPORTANCE OF JOSEPH'S STAND

Joseph knows the outcome of the foolish young man in Proverbs seven who followed the strange woman into her bedchamber. He knows that her ways lead to death and that he will never be able to recover himself fully from such folly. He had made a covenant with his heart that he would not defile himself, violate Potiphar's wife, or cause distrust in his master.

Joseph wasn't exactly elated about having had a slave's garment identification, but his had become that of the top slave. However, he now finds himself back at the place of no identification. The pain is deep; but this time it is different because he left his garment by the choice of his own will. He had learned enough about God's grace and character that he realizes he has made the best choice.

THIS IS OUR STORY

Let us take a short detour here to give hope to those who have not passed temptation's tests with flying colors like Joseph did. There is hope, forgiveness and restoration. At the end of Joseph's story we will see that the brothers who had sold and betrayed the dreamer were forgiven and given the best portion of Egypt.

This is a story not easily told; but because God has moved my husband and myself beyond the past and we are now enjoying the new, we share this testimony.

The temperature hung in the mid-nineties as I tried to find refuge from the tropical heat in our house on the island of Cebu, Philippines. With no cross ventilation or air conditioning, the days could get almost unbearable in the midday heat. I couldn't fault those who found a place, any place…on storefronts, or petty-cab seats…to make into a bed for an afternoon nap.

The heat from without bore down on me, but there was also something within me that was burning as well. My husband and I were like two strangers lost in the night. Our communication had dropped to little more than a rushed "good morning". I couldn't put my finger on what had gone wrong, but he frustrated me and I felt belittled. I was irritated when I asked questions that were ignored and I was angry when the respect I expected wasn't given me.

I counted on him to be up-front with me, but my pent-up emotions that led to outbursts of accusations did nothing to solve our problems. Each time I tried to approach the rift that hung between us, the subject was cunningly diverted and left me defenseless.

Over and over the Lord told me, "Lydia, you're the one who has the problem. You're the one who's angry. You're the one I'm dealing with because you're the object of My love." Once again I would find myself on my knees beside my bed asking forgiveness for my anger. God graciously and lovingly rebuked me until I came to the place of walking in forgiveness.

As time passed the gross sin of my husband's affair was exposed and I was grateful that I had dealt with my anger. Because of that and his confession of the sin committed we were able, with time and perseverance, to resolve issues and receive healing and restoration.

My husband chose to leave the relationship and cleave to me and to our family. He has moved beyond that old life and has found forgiveness, restoration and healing.

One of the lessons my husband says that he learned is that love is a choice and not a feeling. Those who know my husband today see this manifested in his loving lifestyle and strong faith. We rejoice daily for the love we share and the hope we can bring to others.

RESTORATION CAN BE YOURS

So you didn't resist Potiphar's wife! You didn't flee the scene of immorality! Though you had Joseph for an example, you failed to follow it. Now what?

Is there still hope…a way to leave the past behind?

Where do you turn to after you've made this sinful choice?

The answers are:

Turn to God, confessing your sins for what they are! A sin is 'sin' and must be called just that. I John 1:9 says that we must confess our sins. Accept God's forgiveness. The above verse also assures us that God is just and faithful and will forgive us.

Forget what is behind, as Paul admonishes us in Philippians 3:13, and reach for the things that are before us. It is impossible to focus on the past and advance at the same time. Don't confuse your goals by letting your mind dwell on the past.

Begin to focus on the promises of God. Rivet your eyes on who God is! He has given us many things that release us into victorious living!

I John 2:1 tells us we have an advocate. According to Vine's Expository Dictionary, this word depicts a court setting and we are the guilty ones.[2] Our Judge has the capability or adaptability for giving us aid. Christ, as our advocate, denotes the justice who can give us legal assistance, counsel for the defense, and be an intercessor that pleads our cause.

This Advocate sits at the right hand of the Heavenly Father pleading, "Father, I have paid the price for this person's sin. He has repented, so blot out his transgressions."

Our Heavenly Father must then drop the case and vote in our favor.

I Corinthians 1:30 declares that we have redemption. This verse signifies a strong release by the price paid for a ransom. It indicates the deliverance of the believer from the presence and power of sin.

In Colossians 1:13 we see that we have deliverance. Here is what the Amplified Bible says: *"[The Father] has delivered and drawn us to Himself out of the control and dominion of darkness and has transferred us into the kingdom of the Son of His love."*

We're pulled out of the dominion of darkness! Look at what we are transferred into…the kingdom of the Son of His love! So walk away from the sin you gave yourself over to! Square your shoulders and embrace the love of the Son of God! This is your hope and way out.

STAYING MORALLY PURE

We have already talked about what to do if we've blown it. Now let's address the subject of staying morally pure. We have all heard the old saying that says, "An ounce of prevention is better than a pound of cure." This still holds true today! Stay pure! It is easier than to get clean once a person is defiled.

In a world where immorality is the theme of life, it is impossible to speak a strong enough message on moral purity. My heart is crushed when I see that the low moral standard in our churched youth groups barely exceeds that of the world. Where is the pastor, the Bible teacher, the prophet or the youth leader who dares denounce kissing before marriage? Who is holding up the bar of the standard of holiness?

I could write pages to try to persuade my readers that it is imperative for each of our lives to be above reproach, but if we, as people of God, do not make room in our own hearts for purity, these words are in vain. We must come along side each other and admonish one another with godly virtues and values.

The only way we can circumvent the moral decline of our nation is to appropriate God's Word as a standard to live by. I will give you only a short list of guidelines that will become powerful in your life as an overcomer. These keys will work, but only as you make them a constant part of your life. You may well need to enlist a strong Christian friend to walk with you on your journey. Accountability is vital for victory!

- 📖 Start your day with prayer and God's Word. Matthew 6:33

- 📖 Make a vow as David did in Psalm 101:3 not to set any evil thing before his eyes.

- 📖 Abstain from anything that appears to be evil or questionable. I Thessalonians 5:22

- 📖 Make no provisions to fulfill the lusts of the flesh. Romans 13:14

- 📖 Dress to highlight Jesus and not self. I Peter 3:3, 4

- 📖 Flee youthful lusts. II Timothy 2:22

- 📖 Realize that sexual sin is a sin against your own flesh. I Corinthians 6:18

- 📖 Love the Lord with all your heart, soul, mind, strength and you will have no room for lust. Matthew 22:37:40

WHAT PRICE ARE YOU WILLING TO PAY FOR MORAL PURITY?

What price are you willing to pay for moral purity? is the question that needs a personal answer from the heart of each of us. Is it a cost we choose or refuse to pay?

Will we play with sin just a little bit, or will we cut off anything and everything that leads us to moral decline?

Will we flirt, wink, or flaunt ourselves and blame others when the inevitable happens?

Will we blame our parents or someone else for a lack of supervision or training?

Are we willing to assume the responsibility needed to keep ourselves pure?

Will we flee any temptation in order to keep our minds and lives pure?

Are we willing to lose a job, if need be, in order to have an undefiled life?

Do we need to ask if the job we have is a wholesome one?

Will we turn off the TV or eliminate sensual movies and advertisement for the sake of morality?

Have we determined to refuse the wrong kind of music for the sake of moral purity?

Are we willing, as Joseph was, to go to prison for the sake of a clear conscience?

Will we stand for moral purity without considering the cost?

What have we done, and what are we willing to do in order to stay clean before God?

The way we dress makes a strong statement concerning our moral standard. Recently when I was in prayer concerning the immodest apparel that is seen even in our churches the Lord told me; "I am not legalistic, but I also am not immodest." So I ask this also, "What about the way we dress? Are we willing to dress in modest apparel to refute temptation and glorify God?"

I know God is merciful and forgiving, but it's a million times better to stay clean than to need washing after living in the hog wallow of promiscuity and sexual impurity. It is imperative that we keep a clean heart and mind and don't let our conscience become seared with all the evil about us.

GOD REQUIRES PROVING THAT LEADS TO HOLINESS

In these studies we are moving beyond the confines of the flesh to becoming the ultimate church that will be glorious and filled with overcoming strength. The only way that we will begin to ascend to that holy anointing in our lives is by consistently practicing a life of holiness.

Holiness unto the Lord is not legalism. Holiness is freedom from the enslavement to sin. Holiness is a life that is ruled by the Holy Spirit and God's Holy Scriptures! Holiness is separation from things of the world. Holiness will not indulge in the areas of humanistic pursuits listed in I John 2:16. They are:

The lust of the eyes

The lust of our flesh

The pride of life

Joseph fled the scene of immorality and we must follow suit. He was unable to defend himself but in the end God still fulfilled his promises to him.

WHAT WE HAVE DONE

We have understood Joseph's convictions on moral purity.

We have seen him flee from immorality.

We know that it is needful to embrace the fire in order to become refined.

We have been given keys to forgiveness and victory if we are one who has blown it.

We have received keys that will help keep us sexually pure.

We have been challenged to pay a price for moral purity.

AN EXERCISE TO PRACTICE

Memorize Philippians 4:8 "Finally, brethren, whatever things are true, whatever things are noble, whatever things are just, whatever thing are pure, whatever things are lovely, whatever things are of good report, if there is any virtue and if there is anything praiseworthy—meditate on these things."

Write out the type of things you are authorized to think on:

_____

_____

_____

_____

_____

_____

_____

Make a list of things you are willing to do to fortify your pure mind.

_____

_____

_____

_____

_____

_____

_____

_____

_____

_____

The Prison Garb

~ *Genesis 39:20-23* ~

*L*ook, the other slaves are smirking as they watch this handsome Hebrew streak his way to his quarters with less than adequate clothing. They hear the screeches of Potiphar's wife. Her wailing and feigned tears are so real it is almost impossible for anyone not to believe her story of lies. Without further inquiry, the slaves return to their duties and watch for their master's return.

Everyone in the palace knows that Mrs. Potiphar is spending her day in great distress. She has turned her room into a disaster area, and her person is most disheveled. She has made sure that everyone knows her horrible distress, but what about Joseph?

Does anyone know that the young man is innocent, being falsely accused, and praying to the God of his great-grandfather Abraham?

Does anyone care that the top slave could be facing execution before the sun sets?

I can hear Joseph borrow the words of Job in Job 13:15: *"Though He slay me, yet will I trust Him."*

He has spent his day making supplication to his God and examining his own heart to be sure that he has properly dealt with his own soulish issues. By the time Potiphar arrives on the home front and hears his wife's lies, Joseph has worked his way through scriptures into the eighth chapter of Romans. Listen in as he paces the dirt floor in his tiny allotted space. He is speaking the word of God from verses 33 and 34: *"Who shall bring a charge against God's elect? It is God who justifies. Who is he who condemns? It is Christ who died, and furthermore is also risen, who is even at the right hand of God, who also makes intercession for us."*

Joseph reminds God of the dreams he'd given to him years earlier, and then rests his case in the first verse of that chapter. *"There is therefore now no condemnation to those who are in Christ Jesus, who do not walk according to the flesh, but according to the Spirit."*

Joseph has come to grips with his predicament, and peace rules his heart when most of us would coddle the 'I'm scared to death' emotions. Joseph knows that God saw his motives and understands that he fled the site of immorality and fleshly instincts.

Joseph, with his robe of righteousness securely in place, confidently faces the angry, red-faced Potiphar as he arrives at Joseph's quarters. Potiphar's top slave is totally surrounded by peace and submitted to God's will.

Potiphar, who has flown into a rage at his wife's report, could well have Joseph executed without a trial. But God shows His mercy on Joseph's behalf and softens the ruler's revengeful heart.

He hastily thrusts his top slave into the king's prison and rushes back into the arms of his deceitful wife.

THE STAGE IS SET

The stage is set for Joseph. He will either sink or swim in this prison. This is the second time that his garment has been used as lying evidences against him. The first was that beloved colorful coat given to him by his father, but God gave him the grace to leave that behind and move beyond the person he thought he was. He did this without losing his faith in the God of his forefathers.

Next he triumphed as a slave and became the person in charge of all that Potiphar had. Just as he was learning how to serve in that capacity he seemed to suffer another setback. Now he has been given a more demeaning garment to wear—the same garment that all the king's prisoners wore. Joseph is now marked as a criminal without having committed a crime.

The stage is set and even Heaven holds its breath and watches as Joseph enters the king's prison. God pulls back Heaven's curtains and silences the worshipping angels. "I want you to look at that man who is just now entering prison," God informs them. "His name is Joseph and he's the newest kid in that deplorable place. Joseph has just passed some of life's hardest tests and yet more tests await him. When he comes to the end of his life I'll say to him, *"Well done, good and faithful servant."* (Matthew 25:23)

"He was sold into slavery and ruled his life by integrity, honesty and hard work. Then I entrusted him with the trial of his life. It was in the area of moral purity.

As God exposes the sensuality of Mrs. Potiphar the angels all remember that deceitful woman.

Praising Joseph, God continues, "Joseph fled the scene without becoming involved in a tug-of-war to retrieve his garment from her. That was the ultimate test, and Joseph passed it. I am now promoting him to serving Me in prison."

"Promoting?" the angels question in chorus.

God goes on to explain, "I have refined the gold that was in Joseph's human refining vat, but now I am adding one more brick of gold that needs refining. Let's see how he handles serving in prison. If he passes this test I'll know I can entrust him with much of My authority and power!"

"People usually don't think the way that I plan for them to think. They don't realize that my ways are higher than their ways are. They think of trials as a sign that I've forsaken them or that they may have displeased Me and that I am angry with them."

WHAT'S IN IT FOR ME

As we make decisions in life we often ask, "What's in this endeavor for me?" If we invest in a business, we want to be sure that there is something in that investment that will yield returns. In the kingdom of God there are always returns for the investments we make, but many times we do not see them as returns. This is because we do not understand the principles by which God operates.

As we return to Heaven's perspective and listen to the Lord speaking I pray that we will all hear the heartbeat of the Almighty, "My purpose is to refine my children so that they will become overcomers. I am building my church that the gates of hell cannot prevail against. My people must be people of integrity who will serve Me in the least desirable tasks and throughout the darkest hours."

"My people are given challenges so they will learn what is valuable in life. I am using Joseph as an example of adding more gold for the refinement process. In the end these Christians, as Joseph, will have more of My character and authority if they become spiritually exercised by the process."

"If people ask Me, 'What's in it for me?' I will tell them that their strength will be stronger, their faith will be more enduring, their love will grow deeper and My presence will be closer to them because they will become acquainted with Me."

"They need to know that I AM the God who is in each test for them. I AM in each irritation they face. I AM in the hard spots for them. I AM where they are. I AM next to them as they pass through the stormy seas. I AM still the I AM that revealed Himself to Moses in Exodus 3:14."

"I know how much they can endure. I will either remove from their trials the things that are too much for them to bear, or I will give them grace to move through and beyond the test. As they realize I AM there with them they will become my great spiritual warriors to execute My commission."

At this point God closes the curtains of Heaven, and the angels resume their worship with new respect for the Almighty.

WHAT DO YOU DO WHEN YOU'RE AS LOW AS YOU CAN GET?

Is prison as low as we can get? It may well be, and if we find ourselves in some sort of prison we must remember the ultimate love of God. The personal interaction of God's love with us will help us become transformed into the image of Christ and respond to adverse circumstances in a Godly manner.

Joseph's life and the examples of his life reach all the way from the book of Genesis to the book of Revelation. In chapter 3, verse 19 God said, *"As many as I love, I rebuke and chasten. Therefore be zealous and repent."*

Joseph remembered Hebrews 12:11 as he entered the dungeon where Potiphar had secured him. *"Now no chastening seems to be joyful for the present, but painful; nevertheless, afterward it yields the peaceable fruit of righteousness to those who have been trained by it."*

I can hear him further quote I Peter 4:12, 13: *"Beloved, think it not strange concerning the fiery trial which is to try you, as though some strange thing happened unto you: But rejoice, inasmuch as ye are partakers of Christ's sufferings; that, when his glory shall be revealed, ye may be glad also with exceeding joy."* (KJV)

These scriptures do not eliminate the fact that Joseph feels the sting of his demotion, but they help him realize his sufferings were for a specific purpose.

A PERSONAL EXPERIENCE

My dad was involved in many things during my childhood and raising cane and cooking sorghum was one of them. I remember watching him turn the heat up under the vat of raw juices extracted from the sorghum cane plant. The heat brought the impurities to the top so it could be skimmed off and the sorghum purified. I knew when the refiner reached below the vat that it was likely to increase the heat to further refine the product.

During one of the times that I thought my trials were more than I could bear, through divine revelation I saw the Refiner of the gold in my human vat reach below my vat of humanity and turn up the fire another degree.

Instinctively I had cried out, "Oh Lord, no! Not more heat! Not more fire!"

It was then that I realized that it was my Savior, Jesus Christ, who was turning up the degrees of my fire, and as I watched I saw Him skim off the dross of my gold. His loving eyes never averted from the surface of the product He was refining. He was intent on removing all the impurities until He could see His own reflection mirrored in my life—my vat of gold.

Sometime later I learned that the last impurity in gold is silver. When I realized this, it helped me let go of things I felt were of great importance to me. It helped me embrace the fire of my transformation.

WHAT HAPPENS TO JOSEPH NOW?

Confusion, bursts of anger, frustration, complaining, revenge and fear are the usual in Joseph's new home. He has to start from the very bottom. As a new prisoner he has to deal with the lies surrounding his imprisonment—that he tried to rape Mrs. Potiphar. In the middle of the muddle Joseph determines that this will not be his final fate.

He also didn't enter prison as an immature youth who allowed the 'jail-bird' mentality to become his identification. He held onto his dreams and didn't become passive just because he is now shackled and thrust into prison. Nor does he react in an aggressive manner by lashing out at Potiphar in front of the other prisoners.

Joseph has dealt with his anger and isn't out to get revenge and discount anyone's person. He has come to a place where he has learned to welcome pruning, realizing God is fully the God of love, truth and faithfulness.

Joseph's assertiveness had empowered him to execute his chores with dignity and wisdom. Though his demotion to prison placed him among criminals, blasphemers and rebellious outlaws, God has given him grace to minister and serve among the sick and disgruntled.

Joseph understood that the foremost thing of importance is to pursue God's presence. He has not forgotten the covenant of God to his great-grandfather. He has time to remember how God provided a ram for the sacrifice of his grandfather Isaac, how God had visited his father Jacob, and had changed his name to Israel. As Joseph remembers God's faithfulness he begins to align his will with God's.

I don't know how long it took Joseph to become functional in his new surroundings, but before long he realized that he had opportunity knocking all about him. These opportunities were greater than any he had ever encountered before.

Joseph seizes the moment! He prevails with courage in the face of dejected mankind. He dares to smile when others glare at him. He sings when others are cursing. He humbles himself to clean up messes that most skirt with scorn. He learns to speak comforting words to those who haven't heard any kind words since their prison sentence.

As Joseph serves the hurting, he finds that wisdom, insight and managing skills are being imparted to him. He is not timid in making wise suggestions to the prison keeper or stepping into situations that seem unmanageable.

Joseph seeks to promote the wellbeing of those lightly esteemed. As he pours himself into making the prison a better place God entrusts the oversight of that place to him. He is now in charge of the prison—serving in the highest position of the lowest place!

JOSEPH INTERPRETS DREAMS

Genesis 40:4 shows us the serving heart of Joseph. During his prison sentence the king's butler and baker were placed into Joseph's care and "*...he served them...*"

After these two are placed into Joseph's care, he comes to bring them their breakfast, but they have both lost their appetites and seem overly troubled.

"Why are you so sad this morning? The sun is shining outside." Joseph prods with his good-natured personality.

The butler decides to confide in Joseph and tells him about a dream he had that was troubling him. It seemed to have some significance but he couldn't understand it. He's dreamed of a vine with three branches. "The three branches budded and bore fruit, so I picked the grapes and squeezed their juice into Pharaoh's cup," the butler explains.

After acknowledging God as the interpreter of dreams (Genesis 40:8b) Joseph proceeds to tell the butler that Pharaoh will restore him to his butlership in three days.

Now daring to disclose his dream the baker begins, "I was carrying three white baskets on my head. In the top basket I had an assortment of baked goods for Pharaoh. As my dream ended, birds were coming and eating the bread out of my basket."

Joseph speaks with confidence and spiritual insight. "In three days you will be taken from prison and hanged on a tree."

Three days later both the butler and baker's dreams are fulfilled as Joseph had spoken but the butler completely forgets that Joseph had requested him to make mention to Pharaoh concerning himself.

GOD'S TIMING IN EVERYTHING

In his book entitled; *The Joseph Story, Treachery, Betrayal and Redemption*, Ron A. Bishop points out in chapter seven that God's timing is always important and perfect.[1]

Joseph had just been given divine revelation to interpret the dreams of both the butler and the baker, but then Joseph gave in to in own yearning to be removed from the prison he was in. He was in the perfect place, being held secure for the exact time to interpret the next dream.

The thing that happens next shows us how easy it is for us to hear from God in one instant and still make an appeal in the flesh in the next instant. After Joseph had interpreted the dreams he decided to ask a favor of the butler. "When you get out of here, remember me and make request of Pharaoh on my behalf. I was stolen from the land of the Hebrews, and I have done nothing to justify my imprisonment."

The same way that it had been God who had kept Joseph in the confinement of the pit earlier in his life, it was also God who had the butler forget about Joseph until the time for his release.

Two things to be remembered here is the importance of God's timing as well as living our lives according to His timing. We must be careful not to step out of that timing to take charge of things when it is not God's perfect time. *"Having begun in the Spirit, are ye now made perfect by the flesh?"* This is Paul in Galatians 3:3, asking the foolish Galatians to wait on God. We can learn much about God's timing from the great examples in God's Word and especially here in the life of Joseph.

THE TRUTH VERSUS FACTS

The facts in Joseph's life were similar to the facts we face in our own lives. They were defying, denying and deceiving, but the truth was designed, determined and declared by God. We must never believe defying circumstances to be the ultimate outcome for the child of God. The following comparison is worth remembering.

THE FACTS WERE:	THE TRUTH IS:
Joseph was a disregarded prisoner.	He was the beloved son.
Before Joseph got his slave's robe he was stripped bare.	He was clothed with the righteousness of God.
He was alone.	God was always with him.
Nobody knew him.	He was known by God.
He was lied about.	God spoke only the truth to or about him.
His dreams were destroyed.	The dreams were being fulfilled.
Everything had gone wrong.	God was lining up all the events of his life to fulfill his destiny.
He was dead.	He was alive and well.
He was despised, hated and rejected.	He was approved of God to preserve the lineage of the Messiah.
He ached with pain.	He received healing, wellness and respect.
He had immoral desires.	He had fled a lustful situation.
The evidence seemed enough to imprison him.	These were all lying evidences.
He was guilty.	He was pure, guiltless and being proven for approval.
He had been robbed of his identity.	He was learning to recognize his new identity in Christ.
He was forgotten.	He was being preserved in God's time-table.

Consider these four points when you're facing facts that are disagreeing with what the Bible says about you.

Jacob believed the facts.

The brothers gloated over the facts.

Joseph was tested by the facts.

God was in control of the facts.

ALL THE FACTS WERE NEEDED

To bring him to his new location and apart from his earthly father's restrictive doting.

To teach him the virtue of meeting the needs of others through serving them.

To engrain in him the wise management skills needed for his future assignments from God.

To develop faithful responsibility and boldness in him.

To cultivate a lifestyle of forgiveness.

To help him maintain and depend on a close relationship with God.

To cut off soul-ties with those who tried to influence him in an ungodly way and move him beyond the seduction of the Mrs. Potiphars he would be sure to face in the future.

JOSEPH WAS FREE BEHIND BARS

Though these many facts were past experiences in the life of Joseph, consider his freedom:

He was free from guilt and unfaithfulness.

He was free from bitterness and immorality.

He was free from revenge, pride and envy.

He was free from the bondage and condemnation of the past.

He was free to serve and minister to the hurting.

He was free to become Godly and respected as an outstanding prisoner.

He was free to hear from God and increase wisdom.

He was free to learn how to handle hard situations and to triumph over trials.

He was free to be favored by the prison keepers and fellow prisoners.

He was free to exercise discernment and to speak wise counsel.

Someone was out to get Joseph, but God turned the bondage of the bars into a step of surmounting success.

GOD IN THE FACE OF TODAY'S TESTS

If we're going to prevail in our purpose of life and fulfill our destiny, then each of us will face a prison, a wilderness, a desert, a fiery furnace, a captivity, or a cross of some kind.

Jesus is the greatest example of being tested as He hung on the cross, nevertheless each of us have our own prison experiences which are unique and tailored to our own needs. God is there with us in each of our needs.

Modern day miracles are still occurring around the world. My brother, Joe Borntreger, and his wife, Esther, have now been missionaries in Cd Juarez, Mexico for more than 30 years. This city has the infamous label of 'Highest Murder Rate in the World'.

Many ministries are leaving but my brother and sister-in-law affirm that the safest place for them to be is in the center of God's will. On May 29, 2011 God manifested himself and confirmed that these two servants were truly in God's will. During an altar call at their small mission, people were praying around the altar with their heads to the floor.

When Joe heard *"Hermano José"* he looked up from where he was praying and saw a gunman with his pistol pointed at him. With the power and authority of Christ, Joe pointed his finger back at the gunman saying, "There is power in the blood of Jesus." The gunman pulled the trigger repeatedly, but the gun didn't fire.

The lone musician continued to play the guitar and the gunman pulled the trigger again and again, but the gun never fired! Joe pushed the gunman's hand down and he whirled and circled the pews uneasily. Five times he returned and tried to shoot my brother, but Joe's response remained the same, "There is power in the blood of Jesus!" With each pulling of the trigger there was no response from the gun.

As the altar service continued, two ladies, unaware of the immediate danger, prayed loudly in the Spirit. God intervened, confused His enemies and the man with his two companions fled from the building. Once outside the gunman's pistol did fire but he was unable to hurt anyone!

From this testimony we need to realize the greatness of God and the ultimate importance of praying for our missionaries and for each other. Yes, each of us has a test to face, but God is big enough, strong enough and caring enough that He can handle even the most evil situations.

GOD DOESN'T INTEND FOR US TO REMAIN IN PRISON

If God has given us a dream, He didn't intend to leave us in a prison where we can't see it fulfilled. God has plans to bring His people out of their pits, prisons and pandemonium. David says in Psalm 51:8 *"Make me hear joy and gladness, That the bones You have broken may rejoice."*

Our visions should lead us to become broken before God so that in the end we will sing with a voice of joy and gladness. Our broken bones can rejoice for we know that we can triumph through Christ Jesus in spite of our earthly limitations.

Another verse that bears out this concept is Psalm 23:5. *"You prepare a table before me in the presence of my enemies; You anoint my head with oil; My cup runs over."* God does all of these things for us in the presence of our enemies...in our prison cell, if you please! He prepares a table where the fruit of the Spirit

(Galatians 5:22, 23) is lavishly served. He pours out His anointing into our lives and fills our cup with joy!

Job in his distress, after he confessed his unworthiness and prayed for his enemies, had a double restoration of all his possessions and ten beautiful children after his time of affliction.

Jesus' garden of Gethsemane led to His death, but it further led Him to His resurrection. God never intended for Jesus to remain in His grave more than three days. He never intends for us to stay in our pits longer than our allotted processing time. He doesn't want us to die in our prison of selfish living but to abound in His glorious grace. Though Joseph is in prison he's well on his way to becoming a prince over the land.

WHAT YOU HAVE LEARNED

God rejoices when we learn our lessons.

The Refiner (Jesus) always looks for His reflection in our refiner's vat.

The alignment of our will with God's will and timing is a must.

God's truths surpassed the facts in Joseph's life.

All the facts were needed and arranged by God.

Joseph was free in his prison.

You can choose to be free in any prison you find yourself in.

A PRISON EXERCISE TO PRACTICE

It is vitally important for us to learn from the principles governing Joseph's life. If we find ourselves in prison we need to find the purpose and utilize the Word of God for that circumstance. We can all do these spiritual exercises behind our emotional bars until we experience our own freedom in our unique prison.

Let the dying to the flesh be complete. This includes looking beyond this time and space into things of eternal value. II Corinthians 4:18 helps us focus on things with eternal perspective. *"While we do not look at the things which are seen, but at the things which are not seen. For the things which are seen are temporary, but the things which are not seen are eternal."*

Learn who your real enemy is, and don't strike out against the people around you. Thoroughly acquaint yourself with Ephesians 6:12. *"For we do not wrestle against flesh and blood, but against principalities, against powers, against the rulers of the darkness of this age, against spiritual hosts of wickedness in the heavenly places."*

Serve with gladness in the lowest capacity. See Matthew 25:21b: *"you were faithful over a few things, I will make you ruler over many things."*

Seize every opportunity that presents itself to you. Remember most of these opportunities wear a disguise and should remind us of Matthew 25:40. *"And the king will answer and say to them, 'Assuredly, I say to you, inasmuch as you did it to one of the least of these My brethren, you did it to Me.'"*

Turn to God with every trial. I Peter 5:7 commands us, *"Casting all your care upon Him, for He cares for you."*

Let go of the past ...the good, the bad and the indifferent. As long as we try to resurrect our yesterday's pleasant memories, we can't enjoy today's sweet scent of roses. In my case, I had to let go of my glowing title of being an overseas missionary in order to embrace this privilege of serving my disabled husband. Paul let go of his past. In Philippians 3:7-9 he says, *"But what things were gain to me, these I have counted loss for Christ. Yet indeed I also count all things loss for the excellence of the knowledge of Christ Jesus my Lord, for whom I have suffered the loss of all things, and count them as rubbish, that I may gain Christ*

The Garment of Transition

~ *Genesis 41:14* ~

*T*he floor is hard beneath Joseph's thin mat in his tiny prison cell. The night is still pitch black, and the air thick with dingy smells of a dungeon. But something is different, Joseph feels warm and comforted as he reaches for wakefulness.

It is the morning after the butler and the baker's dreams have been fulfilled. Word has filtered back into the prison that the butler has been restored to his office as Pharaoh's cupbearer and that the baker has been hanged.

"Where am I?" he mumbles to himself.

Then he realizes, no, I'm not the teenager that brought the tales of my brothers' misconducts to my father. I'm not back in the land of the Hebrews, and I'm still in this dungeon.

It takes a minute before Joseph is fully aware of the time, the place and the dreams he has just dreamed. "How strange! How impossible!" Joseph whispers to himself. "I dreamed these same dreams years ago. I had almost forgotten how lusciously golden the eleven sheaves were which bowed down to my sheaf. And then just as in the dreams of my youth, I saw the open heaven with eleven stars, the moon and the sun bowing down to my star. How can it be that I've dreamed these same dreams over again? It must be that God will surely fulfill His promises even after all these years."

Urgency seizes the heart of the twenty-nine year old who is no longer an inexperienced and carefree youth, but now a man of maturity. He had overcome many things in his world turned upside-down but now he realizes that there is a spiritual war which he must win through intercession with thanksgiving.

JOSEPH PREVAILS IN PRAYER

"Oh, God of my great-grandfather, Abraham, hear me now in this prison cell. You have spoken to me in my youth. You visited me while I was immature and careless with my lifestyle. I have repented of my arrogance and received Your forgiveness. I have learned integrity and cultivated Your characteristics in my daily life."

"Almighty Lord, how will You bring these dreams to pass?"

Joseph's prayer vigil, long and intense, prevails until daybreak. As the dawn breaks on the horizon there is a spiritual breakthrough as he remembers God's exhortation in Jude verse three. *"Beloved, while I was very diligent to write to you concerning our common salvation, I found it necessary to write to you exhorting you to contend earnestly for the faith which was once for all delivered to the saints."*

He had earnestly contended and Joseph's faith is renewed. God has reaffirmed his mission and urges him to step into the spiritual realm of intercession and thanksgiving. It will take the power of

God to prevail against the darkness of the present world which keeps him imprisoned.

INTERCESSION BRINGS SPIRITUAL REVELATION

In a way, you and I are also in Joseph's prison where we too have not seen our God-given purposes totally fulfilled in our lives. It is necessary for us to learn from Joseph as he prays. Look, God is bringing him revelation that will move him beyond this prison to the fulfillment of God's promises to him. He must encounter spiritual warfare to move beyond the boundaries of the flesh.

Realizing that to live after the flesh brings death, he also knows that 'Christ in us' brings life. (Romans 8:12, 13) He recognizes that he must put off the deeds of the body and the flesh in order to live. This means a transformation—a changed life and heart. Joseph can no more stand before the majestic ruler of Egypt in a prisoner's garb, than we can stand before the King of Kings clothed in our own righteousness. (Isaiah 64:6) The prisoner's garment will never do. A robe of transition must be purchased. Joseph prays for favor and goes to the prison master.

"I have dreamed again the dreams of my youth," Joseph explains. "I am here to make an appeal of you. Please Sir, allow me just one hour to go to the market and purchase the robe I will need for my release from prison." The request was made in faith and he rests his case with God.

The prison master was speechless for a moment, "This type of request is never granted, but I'll bring the matter to the king and will inform you later on what he says."

Joseph realizes that it will literally take God to fulfill His promises.

Many times during the day Joseph repeats II Corinthians 10:3-6; *"For though we walk in the flesh, we do not war according to the flesh. For the weapons of our warfare are not carnal but mighty in God for pulling down strongholds, casting down arguments and every high thing that exalts itself against the knowledge of God, bringing every thought into captivity to the obedience of Christ, and being ready to punish all disobedience when your obedience is fulfilled."*

As we observe the steadfastness of Joseph's prevailing prayers, we must also intercede for our own manifested transformation. Days pass as Joseph prevails in prayer, asking for his release to buy a new robe. His prayers turn to confessions of faith and thanksgiving. At night he sleeps soundly and each day awakens with expectation of what God will do.

He executes his tasks in a joyful manner while he recites Romans 12:11, *"not lagging in diligence, fervent in spirit, serving the Lord."* He realizes that the butler has forgotten about him and no longer expects men to bring his release, but his eyes are fastened on God. He knows God has not forgotten him.

Joseph's vision is an important part of his prayer life and a key to obtaining his robe of transition. Joseph knows that if he has no vision, no progressive, ongoing and redemptive revelation of God, the people God has ordained for him to rescue will perish. (Proverbs 29:18)

JOSEPH'S REQUEST IS GRANTED

Joseph's request is finally granted, and his heart is soaring. He knew God would bring to pass his request and he would not be distracted from the pursuit of his vision. *"Faith without works is dead,"* (James 2:26) are the words ringing in his heart as he goes to the markets for a robe suitable for his release at the appointed hour.

He knows his allotted hour will pass quickly as he searches the open market for just the right robe. God has shown him the type of robe he'll need to stand before Pharaoh at the time appointed.

"It must be the equivalent of the Hebrew's meil-type clothing," Joseph tells himself. As he steps into the last little shop at the end of the market, he spots the robe God had shown him. He pays the clerk, who is eyeing him in surprise.

"First time I've ever sold one of these beautiful garments to a jailbird," he muses.

Joseph ignores the comment and hurriedly returns to the prison within his allotted hour. He has taken one more step of faith and has done everything humanly possible to prepare for his physical release. This brings a deep sense of assurance and God's peace comforts him.

FAITH, THE UNEXPLAINABLE

How can one explain faith when it is the substance of unseen things? How can one understand faith when it is evidence that the human mind cannot comprehend?

Hebrews 11 is the "Faith Chapter." It contains God's "Hall of Fame," listing many Old Testament saints who through faith obtained the promises God had given. Hebrews 11 also gives us insight into what faith is and how it works. Verse one declares, *"Now faith is…"* Faith exists now! It is evident at this present time. Faith is the substance and evidence of the unseen! Bright minds and human logic cannot explain the tenor, meaning or essence of faith, and yet it becomes the believer's guide.

Verse six says we must have faith in order to please God. It is totally illogical but not evasive or non-purposeful. Faith is a substance of the spirit-portion of humanity. It bypasses the human mind and reaches beyond reason. It's God-given demand reaches further than the sphere of human thinking, understanding or intelligence.

Because God is God, He doesn't have to make sense to our finite minds, but He must be believed in and responded to. He is the great Creator of heaven and earth, and we could never understand just how He created a leaf or flower petal. These are creations formed by the power of His Word and surpass human understanding or ability to duplicate.

Since pleasing God hinges on faith, we must know how to obtain faith. Romans 10:17 holds our key: *"So then faith comes by hearing, and hearing by the word of God."* The key is to hear God's Word in our spirit, rather than by our carnal mind. When we hear the Lord's voice speak to us, it demands a response of faith.

Contrary to our carnal thinking, the grass is not greener on the other side of the fence unless, as some say, it is growing over a cesspool! Through the eyes of faith it is the greenest right here and now. This moment of 'now' is the time to dig into God's Word, increase our faith and grow in Christ-likeness. Here our faith can take wings and bring us to our own place of transformation!

It took faith, in the life of Joseph, for him to obtain his robe of transition. It took faith for him to keep it clean and unwrinkled in a vile jail cell. When we are in a place that seems less desirable than other places we've been in, or less enjoyed than places our friends seem to be enjoying, it is time to let faith walk with us.

Faith lets us know God's grace is sufficient for these times of testing! Unwavering faith teaches us to say, "I am strong" when we feel weak. It turns the little we have into the makings for a miracle. It takes what God entrusts to us, and hands it right back to Him to see what He will do with it. Faith turns our bread crumbs into living bread. It changes our cries to songs and worship.

PATIENCE JOINS FAITH'S PURSUITS

Contrary to what some may think, patience doesn't hamper faith's progress. Patience isn't passive and doesn't mumble, "Well, whatever."

Joseph's long years of testing reached a peak after he interpreted the butler's dream. This was a time when his faith turned into a lifestyle of trust as he exercised patience. As Joseph reminded himself of his need for patience, I can see him journaling the following in his heart:

"Through assertiveness, patience pursues my vision! It is linked with endurance and encouraged by the overcomer's mindset. Patience ensues and prevails to the end. It's not discouraged by carrying the tiny load of an ant, for it continues it's journeys until the task is accomplished. It avails itself of the opportunities at hand rather than sitting back lethargically and lacking endurance."

"Patience never complains about carrying heavy loads. It doesn't whine when the travels are long, the goings get rough, the sun is suffocating, or the puzzle pieces don't fit. Patience leans on faith when the hill seems too long for the energy at hand and doesn't concern itself with those who move on up ahead of it."

"Patience savors the present without reaching for tomorrow's gems. It takes time to heal the hurting, wipe away tears, and speak words of comfort. Patience paces itself without laziness or anxiety."

"In my patience I must never allow the following in my thought-patterns:

I have failed.

I'm not going to try anymore.

It's not worth the efforts or the price.

I'm too tired to wait any longer.

I can't do this.

Joseph finished his journal entry with "Though those delinquent thoughts have tried to lodge in my mind, I will not permit this. I choose to live by faith, exercising the patience of my forefathers, and I will pursue my dreams."

What seemed like a cruel time slot in prison actually provided him the opportunity to turn his adverse situations into a period for healing. He allowed the pride of others to make him humble. He permitted the assault of his fellow prisoners to make him assertive as he personalized Isaiah 54:17: *"No weapon formed against me will prosper…"* God's promises retained became his entrance to forthcoming fame.

I AM A RECIPIENT

Joseph's mentality had to be completely transformed from his natural reaction to facts, into responding rightly to God's declared truths. Rather than replaying the 'vivid videos of recall,' he punched the eject button and put in a video called 'The Grace of God.' As he replayed God's mercy and grace in his life, words of gratitude well up in his heart:

I am a recipient of God's grace…His everlasting love.

I am a recipient of redemption, freedom, and forgiving mercy.

I'm a recipient of enduring truth, joy and peace.

I am a recipient of justification and wisdom that far transcends my own.

I am a recipient of God's righteousness and sanctification.

I am a recipient of His eternal life and holiness.

I am a recipient of His graciousness and triumphant victory.

Christ suffered all for me, and I'm a recipient of all I need.

PHARAOH'S URGENT SUMMONS ARRIVES

My heart is pumping with excitement as we crowd into a corner of Joseph's tiny cell to see what will happen next. I know that you also sense the air of expectancy!

Joseph is still focusing on God's goodness when his quiet meditation is shattered by an urgent voice crying into his stockade, "Where is Joseph, the Hebrew prisoner?"

Joseph's heart skips a beat, as he seems to recognize a familiar voice from his past. Guards at the gate quickly work to resolve the ruckus created by the unexpected visitor.

The voice booms again, "Where is Joseph? Pharaoh, the king of Egypt, has sent me to summon him. The command is urgent and immediate!"

"Yes, that is a familiar voice," Joseph muses to himself, but it isn't until he gets a glimpse of the messenger himself that he fully realizes it is Potiphar, the man who'd thrown him into prison.

Now the guard's voice joins with the messenger of Pharaoh, "Come on out here, Joseph. The king has a job for you to do. Just come this way, and I'll unlock the gate, and you can be on your way."

Joseph pushes his way through the mass of inmates to find out just what is expected of him.

"You must go with Potiphar to see what the king wants," the guard commands.

Joseph is not so inclined. "Sir, in my expectation of this call I've purchased a robe to change into for the time of my appearance before the king. I cannot go into the king's presence with this unacceptable prison garb. Please kindly excuse me to go and change."

Joseph is confident this is his time to step beyond the confines of this prison. However, he is also challenged by the presence of the man who had thrown him into prison on the basis of a lie.

As he changes his prisoner's robe for the meil-type coat, he searches his heart for any unforgiveness that might lurk in some dark corner. He shaves off his beard to be accepted by the Egyptian king and splashes on a bit of the special sweet-scented oil that he keeps for special occasions. A deep peace settles over him. He knows he's been forgiven and that he has forgiven this man who seemingly wronged him.

Joseph steps from his prison onto the damp stony stairway leading toward the palace. Because Joseph had dealt with unforgiveness, pride, arrogance, blame and self-centeredness while in his prison cell, he is able to walk from that dank dungeon without any extra soul-junk.

When Potiphar explains to Joseph that the reason for Pharaoh's summon is that he had dreamed dreams that troubled him, Joseph isn't concerned about God's ability to give the king a peaceful answer. He also knows that God will give him the ability to deliver the Word of the Lord to Pharaoh. He doesn't waste any of his first precious moments out of prison with fretfulness or worry; instead Joseph softly whispers as he climbs the stairway out of his confinement.

Psalm 115:15: *"Ye are blessed of the LORD which made heaven and earth."* (KJV)

Psalms 23:6: *"Surely goodness and mercy shall follow me all the days of my life; and I will dwell in the house of the LORD forever."* (KJV)

Since Joseph had availed himself of his favorite 'freedom packet' of Romans 8, he recalls the reassuring verses of 35-39.

"Who shall separate us from the love of Christ? Shall tribulation, or distress, or persecution, or famine, or nakedness, or peril, or sword? As it is written: For Your sake we are killed all day long; We are accounted as sheep for the slaughter."

"Yet in all these things we are more than conquerors through Him who loved us. For I am persuaded that neither death nor life, nor angels nor principalities nor

powers, nor things present nor things to come, nor heights nor depth, nor any other created thing, shall be able to separate us from the love of God which is in Christ Jesus our Lord."

By now Joseph has a spring in his step, a song in his heart, confidence pumping through his veins, and his head lifted by strong, squared shoulders.

A great peace engulfs him as he recalls the promise and the command of Jesus in John 14:27. *"Peace I leave with you, my peace I give to you; not as the world gives do I give to you. Let not your heart be troubled, neither let it be afraid."*

Besides gaining confidence from Scripture, Joseph also knows his robe of transition speaks of wisdom, assertiveness and approachability. It was neither overbearing nor degrading. This stability keeps him steady and calm as he faces the biggest challenge of his life. His countenance radiates an inner assurance that attracts Pharaoh to him.

JOSEPH'S EXPERIENCE CAN ENCOURAGE YOU

Earlier in this chapter we saw ourselves in our own prison as we saw Joseph in his. Can you now think of a time when you've had dreams and inspiration that you set up on a shelf of doubt somewhere due to circumstances beyond your control?

Do you find yourself identifying with Joseph's prison experience?

Just as his life seemed to have ended up in an impossible situation with his long years of imprisonment, so you may feel you are at the end of your hopes and dreams. But remember that

Joseph's unjust prison sentence was only the beginning of his life. The two extra years added to his stay in prison after interpreting the butler's dreams were all a vital part of God's timing. It was God confining him to His time line. If you find yourself in an overwhelming situation, meditate on the following Kingdom truths:

There is no door closed so tightly that it cannot be opened.

There is no destiny so destroyed that it cannot be restored.

There is no situation so discouraging that God's Word can't encourage it.

There is no pain or heartbreak so deep that it cannot be healed.

There is no prison so confining that its prisoners cannot be freed.

There are no issues so defiant that they cannot be resolved.

There is no night so dark that it can prevent the day.

There are no needs so great that they cannot be met.

There is no end so final that eternity doesn't hold its answer.

The account in Acts 16:25 of Paul and Silas singing God's praises in prison is an example of being free even in captivity. As they sang, God sent an earthquake and physically released them. God wants His people to be free to abound in Him.

WHAT YOU HAVE LEARNED

God wants us to remember our God-given dreams.

We must prepare our hearts for transition by earnestly contending for God's promises to be fulfilled in our lives.

Faith is an unseen, unexplainable substance that brings results in the believers' lives.

Faith comes by hearing the Word of God.

We must have our lives transformed by patience and trust.

Faith lets us know that God's grace is sufficient for our times of testing and bringing us release from our prison.

Faith and patience are partners that encourage each other.

Joseph had an 'I am a recipient' mentality.

There is no problem so big that it cannot be resolved.

AN EXERCISE TO PRACTICE

Psalm 23:5 says, *"You prepare a table before me in the presence of my enemies; You anoint my head with oil; My cup runs over."* Here are two questions for us to ask concerning this verse.

1. Why would God prepare a table for us and sit us down in the presence of our enemies to feed us?

2. What kind of food would God prepare for us and serve to us?

Since God is Spirit and He feeds us spiritually, I believe we will find the kind of food that God feeds us in Galatians 5:22 and 23. Here we see that He prepares a table where the fruit of the Spirit is lavishly served to His children. As we study the following concepts, it is important to note where love is best served. We can see that joy is most precious in a gloomy atmosphere. When we realize all these virtues are ours to partake of in the face of our own difficulties, we will understand why God spreads His table for us in the presence of our enemies.

- To <u>love</u> our enemies is Christ's command. Matthew 5:44

- <u>Joy</u> comes after the night of sorrow. Psalm 30:5

- <u>Peace</u> is for our time of trouble. John 14:27

- <u>Longsuffering</u> is to be expected by ministers. II Corinthians 6:4-6

- <u>Gentleness</u> is an aspect of wisdom. James 3:17

- <u>Goodness</u> leads to repentance. Romans 2:4

- <u>Faith</u> is needful if we will please God. Hebrews 11:6

- <u>Meekness</u> is a requirement in obtaining our inheritance. Matthew 5:5

- <u>Temperance</u> is needed in our aging process. Titus 2:2 (References taken from KJV)

Write down the 9 fruits of the Spirit and memorize them. Pray for these to become your robe of transformation as you face the challenges of each new day.

    1. _____

    2. _____

    3. _____

4. _____

5. _____

6. _____

7. _____

8. _____

9. _____

We must hold onto these virtues by faith in Jesus Christ until we are transformed during each phase of our lives.

The Royal Robe of Authority

~ Genesis 41:37-45 ~

*L*ook, there's Joseph now! He's beckoning for us to experience this miracle with him! If we hurry we can fall into step beside him.

At the time Joseph is being summoned to the palace, Egypt is a highly modernized society with much idolatry and sophisticated temples. Vast columns yield their strength to the structure as Joseph climbs the stairs of Pharaoh's majestic palace.

The expanse of hallways seems endless to Joseph as he walks next to Potiphar; and the two make their way to Pharaoh's throne room. The echoes of their footsteps precede them, and guards and servants stand aside as the pair step through the arched doorway into the king's presence.

Pharaoh's dynasty represents ultimate power in this highly developed society. The parliaments of legislature and great wisdom have come from this dictator. He represents the humanistic philosophy of a self-made man who lacks divine wisdom.

When the God of Abraham stepped in, Pharaoh's wisdom suddenly ended and the great ruler sits baffled and completely defeated! His inability to interpret his dreams has eroded his self-security until he sits slouched, with his head in his hands, staring off into space. As Joseph gets his first glimpse of Pharaoh he looks more like a madman than the brilliant king he is. The sight strikes home the realization that Egypt's highest source of wisdom has seemingly been defeated.

Pharaoh's dreams have tormented him with sleeplessness. He is distraught because his wise men have failed to interpret them. The butler's forgetfulness in mentioning Joseph has further agitated him. Pharaoh's rage has struck fear of execution into the hearts of the wisest princes in Egypt.

Potiphar is not exempt from the fears that the others are experiencing. He trembles as he realizes he is chosen to bring Joseph from the prison in which he had thrown him years earlier. The hazy details of the earlier event turn into a clear focus. Suddenly he realizes he'd condemned an innocent man and come into wrong agreements with his wife. His prideful heart is doing a fast meltdown.

THE DREAMS INTERPRETED

Joseph and Potiphar stand in total silence until Pharaoh speaks, "Is this the man you've brought to interpret my dreams?" he demands angrily of Potiphar.

"Yes-s-s, Your-r-r Highness, this is Joseph whom the butler spoke of," stammers Potiphar. The whole turn of events in Potiphar's life has left him uncertain of his future.

Now the king's attention shifts to Joseph. He takes a moment to assess the man who stands before him. His eyes meet Joseph's and the king sees a warmth and depth in them that commands him to entrust him with his dreams. The fear of baring his soul to a jailbird is completely gone.

He begins, "I hear that you can interpret dreams. Is that correct?"

Joseph's confidence remains undaunted as he answers with a steady voice. "Your Majesty, I am not the One who can interpret your dreams, but I know the One who interprets all dreams. This giver of dreams will give Pharaoh an answer of peace."

Eager to hear the answer to the thing that distresses him, Pharaoh begins to elaborate on his dreams.

"I cannot shake myself from the reality of my dreams! I was standing on a riverbank that was lush and flourishing. I sensed the breeze blowing in my face, and the sun was warm on my head. As I looked at the peaceful rippling of the water there suddenly appeared seven well-fed cows. These robust cows walked onto the shore and started grazing. The last one no sooner got to shore, when suddenly out of nowhere, seven skinny cows appeared."

"I've never seen such horrible looking creatures. These ill-favored cows were obviously starving because they ate up all the fattened cows without leaving any evidence that they had ever existed."

"I was disturbed by my awful dream but dismissed it and finally dozed off into another fitful sleep. Again I dreamed a dream similar to the first. I was amazed as I watched a stalk of corn grow beyond any heights I'd ever seen! It produced seven full ears of luscious corn unlike anything Egypt has ever seen."

"As I was admiring this stalk of corn there suddenly appeared seven ears of bad corn. Blasted by the wind, these ears were scrawny and more poorly developed than any I've ever seen before!"

"I couldn't believe what I was looking at when I saw the blasted ears eat the fat ears of corn without leaving a trace of the first ones."

Joseph, sensing this ended the king's dialogue, bows his head in reverence to the God of Heaven. After a moment of silence he confidently lifts his head and shifts his position to address Pharaoh. Without any airs he squares his shoulders and interprets both dreams.

"The dreams are about the same thing. The first seven cows and fat ears of corn represent seven years of plenty in Egypt. The next seven are seven years of desperate famine that will ensue. For the next seven years the earth will produce an abundant harvest, but the following seven years will be years of dire famine. These will be so severe that nobody will remember there'd been years of plenty. The Lord doubled the dream to Pharaoh so your Highness will know that God has spoken it and it will surely come to pass."

Pharaoh sits speechless for a long moment, and Joseph takes advantage of the opportunity to speak further.

"Your Highness, I will tell the king what he must do. You must find a man in your kingdom who is good with people, who has a business mind, and who will be a faithful servant. Set that man over the affairs of the land, and let him select officers who will gather into storehouses the excess of the years of plenty so you'll have food during the years of famine."

Pharaoh realizes that Joseph has not only interpreted the dreams, but has also spoken a word of wisdom to him. Suddenly the desperate king squares his shoulders and summons all his wise men.

"Look at this man," he demands of them all. "This man was just released from jail half an hour ago, and he has already interpreted my dreams for me. He has also given me a word of wisdom so I may know how to handle this crucial time for our land. He is filled with the Spirit of the living God. Can we find anyone his equal?"

Pharaoh then turned to Joseph and said, "I can see that God has given you a channel of understanding that neither I nor any of the governors possess. There is none that is as discreet and wise as you are! I will promote you to be over my house with special authority in the land. You will be my chief advisor as a father is to his son."

The king's court, now speechless; nod their heads in consent. How could they disagree? Joseph had saved their lives.

At this Joseph bows to his knees before the Almighty One who instructed him. In this he also shows reverence and a positive response to Pharaoh.

As the full impact of what has just taken place hits Potiphar, he leans over to the butler and whispers, "This can only be an act of a God who is superior to our gods."

GOD SUMMONS US TO COME INTO HIS PRESENCE

Since we're keeping in step with Joseph, it's relevant that we understand how this step of release and promotion in his life relates to us. God is summoning us to come and spend time in His presence. It is as we heed His beckoning that He promotes us to our place of spiritual authority.

No matter where we find ourselves in this dialogue of Joseph's life, the invitation to come into God's presence applies to all of us. We will look at some Scriptures to see who may come before the throne of God.

- 📖 Isaiah 1:18 calls for those with sins as scarlet to come for a cleansing.

- 📖 Isaiah 55:1 summons anyone who is spiritually thirsty to come for a satisfying portion of God's presence.

- 📖 Matthew 11:28 invites those who are weary and loaded down with heaviness to come for rest in their soul.

- 📖 Matthew 22:4 invites all that are bidden to the feast to come to the King's banquet.

- 📖 Revelation 22:17 bids anyone who desires to come and take of the water of life to come and drink freely.

Jesus Christ, the door into God's presence, welcomes all ages, colors, and nationalities. Denominational barriers cannot bar anyone from God's presence. We must come daily into His dwelling place so He can entrust us with more of His anointing.

ONE DAY IN THE LIFE OF JOSEPH

Joseph's first day in the palace had started much like any other of his days in prison. With the squeaking hinges of the jail cell doors and the moaning complaints of the prisoners, he had awakened at dawn, acknowledging the God of his forefathers. He had sought direction for his day and prayed again for the butler's memory to be jarred as he inspected his robe of transition.

At that moment he had heard a commotion at the guard's gate, and within minutes he was interpreting the king's dreams and advising him. It had only taken a short portion of his day to walk through the door that had remained locked to him for his long years in the king's dungeon. God's timing, faith and patience had awakened Joseph in prison before sunrise and tucked him into the bed of a palace that same night.

Joseph's heart had been prepared in prison to assume the responsibility of a palace. It didn't take God even twenty-four hours to completely rearrange his life and bring him to the position where he'd later see his dreams fulfilled. One day had made the difference in Joseph's life from him being in the confines of jail to being a ruling prince of Egypt's palace.

COMPARING JOSEPH'S GIFTS TO THOSE IN THE CHURCH

The gifts of Pharaoh to Joseph are found listed in Genesis 41:39-45. It is important for us to see these gifts in the light of the gifts that God has given to His church. Bethlehem's babe gave us the Savior of the world, but this Savior has also imparted to us the Holy Spirit which is manifested in various and special gifts in and to the church.

Fine Linen Garment

It isn't hard for Joseph to leave his robe of transition for the white linen robe that carries great significance and authority. The robe Pharaoh gives him is a robe that sets him apart as the second ruler in the land of Egypt. It is a flawless vesture of fine linen, bleached to a pure white.

As Joseph caresses the robe's smoothness he realizes that its significance of authority far exceeds the authority that his coat of many colors had carried. The significance of the two couldn't be compared. The coat of his youth identified him as the head over his father's household back in Canaan, but this intricately woven garment sets him apart as a ruler over all of Egypt.

This spiritual attire is comparable to the meil-type clothing of the Hebrews—representing the authority that God gives to His people. We can readily see this difference if we look at the life of Peter.

In John 13:37 Peter tells the Lord that he will lay down his life for His sake. There is no doubt concerning Peter's intent to be faithful to Christ, but when we look at Luke 22 we will see the drowsiness in Peter that lended itself to sleep when the Lord asked him to keep a prayer vigil. Then we will see that after Jesus was arrested Peter followed them, but at a distance he esteemed to be safe. In verses 55-62 we see Peter's denial of the One he had vowed to die for. He swore that he didn't know the man.

Was this the end of Peter? Did this leader of Christ's apostles fail too miserably to be restored and reinstated to God's call in his life? Actually the answer to these questions is "NO!" He had on his robe of righteousness, but he lacked power to stand up for the Lord.

In Acts 2:14 we see that Peter is back on the scene. This time he is boldly proclaiming the Christ that was crucified and resurrected. In order for us to understand the difference in the significance of Joseph's colorful coat and the fine linen garment, we need to understand what transpired between the time of 'Peter-the-coward' and 'Peter-the emboldened'.

There are three things that happened between these two time periods.

Peter repented. He went out and wept bitterly. (Luke 22:62)

Jesus re-commissioned Peter. (John 21:15-17)

He was filled and empowered with the Holy Spirit. (Acts 2:4)

As the first Peter he already believed in Christ, which we have portrayed as wearing God's robe of Righteousness, yet he still lacked the boldness which he received in Acts two. The resurrected Lord Jesus Christ had promised this power in Acts 1:8. *"But you shall receive power when the Holy Spirit has come upon you; and you shall be witnesses to Me in Jerusalem, and in all Judea and Samaria and to the end of the earth."*

Peter's three-step restoration brought him to the place where he could impart to us the completion of the concept of Joseph's glorious linen garment—our own restoration to the fulfillment of Christ's desire for us. In Ephesians 5:27 Peter expresses that desire: *"that He might present her to Himself a glorious church, not having spot or wrinkle or any such thing, but that she should be holy and without blemish."*

This Spirit-of-God-filled life is one of the first gifts that the Lord gave to His Church after His ascension. It is that linen garment of spiritual authority and godly manifestation that Christ wants us to wear today.

The King's Ring

The account of Pharaoh giving Joseph his ring is one of the earliest recordings of the significance of the ring. The ring, as a symbol of authority, is seen several times throughout the Bible. The Hebrew word for ring is *tabbaath* and means to sink or stamp.

Early on the ring became very valuable as shown by Isaiah's plaint recorded in Isaiah 3:18-23. These rings, found among Hebrew artifacts, were engraved stones and were first worn on chains around the neck. For safety however, the ring was later transferred to the finger.[1]

In today's society, the wedding ring may most closely relate to this exchange of rings. Exchanging rings is a gesture of the groom giving his bride his name, his provisions, his care and his loving devotion. She steps into a new arena of life and identification by taking on her husband's name.

In the same way, the church is given the Name of Jesus as a symbol of spiritual authority. Jesus assures us of this truth in John 14:14, *"If you ask anything in My name, I will do it."*

Matthew 17:20 declares, *"...for assuredly, I say to you, if you have faith as a mustard seed, you will say to this mountain, 'Move from here to there,' and it will move; and nothing will be impossible for you."*

Jesus longs for us to avail ourselves of the spiritual authority that is legally ours in His name. Joseph, knowing the authority the king's ring represented, took it and stepped into his position of a ruler. We too are to use the authority of Christ's name in a wise way, doing all we do in the name of Jesus. (See Colossians 3:17)

As Joseph looked out for the welfare, safety and preservation of the Pharaoh and the land of Egypt, so we must diligently avail ourselves to our authority in Christ, and become effective ministers of God's grace to all that He leads us to do.

Gold Chain of Distinction

Chains in Scripture are sometimes mentioned as an ornament such as a necklace, but they are also used as fetters. In this setting, however, the gold chain is the equivalent of a distinguished service medal bestowed by the ruler of a state and signifying specific honor.[2]

This mark of distinction corresponds with Psalm 4:3: *"But know that the LORD has set apart for Himself him who is godly;"*

We are a distinguished people set apart for the Lord and for the infilling of His Holy Spirit. Peter bears this out in I Peter 2:9: *"But you are a chosen generation, a royal priesthood, a holy nation, His own special people, that you may proclaim the praises of Him who called you out of darkness into His marvelous light."*

Joseph was in Egyptian culture but he dared not make himself of the people. He was above the groveling and complaining of the flesh. He had connections to the anointing that opened precise doors of direction for the land. He was walking in an anointing that broke his yoke of bondage. (Isaiah 10:27) Similarly we are set apart, being in the world without being of the world.

A New Name

Rachel, Joseph's mother, had been barren for many years while her sister was giving birth to Jacob's sons. Genesis 30 tells us that God remembered Rachel's cry and gave her a son whom she named Joseph, meaning, 'let Him add'. Pharaoh renamed Joseph feeling that Zaphnath-pa-a-neah suited him better.

Zaphnath-pa-a-neah means 'the one who furnishes the substance of the land'[3] and signifies the trust Pharaoh had in Joseph. He knew Joseph's God was superior to any of the gods in Egypt.

In essence Pharaoh was saying, "God had already added to Joseph and now he needs to be recognized as the provider of Egypt."

Joseph, now seen as an overcomer, links us to Revelation 2:17; *"He who has an ear, let him hear what the Spirit says to the churches. To him who overcomes I will give some of the hidden manna to eat. And I will give him a white stone, and on the stone a new name written which no one knows except him who receives it."*

The two points I want to make here are that we're called to be overcomers and that God wants us to have a new name. God wants us to triumph in our trials and exercise our faith in the face of fear. This gives us the grace of an overcomer and prepares us for the new name God has for us.

God's choice of names for us will be astounding and we wouldn't recognize ourselves by it here on earth. God's kingdom insights far surpass our earthly concepts, and He knows us better than we know ourselves.

A Bride

Joseph has waited many years for a wife, and the days that follow his release from prison lead him to a hurried introduction to his bride-to-be and her family. He has guarded his moral purity and left any marriage plans in the hands of God. Now he is given the beautiful daughter of Potipherah, priest of On, to wife.[4]

Though Joseph's marriage grants him prestige among the elite in Egypt, it also has its downside. This marriage makes him the son-in-law of Potipherah, who is the high priest of the idolatrous paganism of Egypt. The city of On is a terminus of numerous caravan routes, and the Sun-god centered there has peculiar features that suggests the influence of Syria. Joseph finds himself thrust into the middle of the whole scene of commerce and paganism that we wouldn't normally deem a positive spiritual influence.[5]

Joseph's marriage to a pagan wife is again a matter completely beyond Joseph's control, but one God uses. Because of Joseph's union with Asenath, two important figures in the lineage of Jesus were born: Manasseh and Ephraim.

An amazing parallel is drawn here between Joseph and Asenath's marriage and the spiritual marriage of Jesus Christ and His bride, the church. As Asenath was from pagan roots, so we were born in sin and shaped in iniquity. It was while we were yet in our sins that Christ died for us. He did this so that He might present to Himself a glorious, spotless church. In Ephesians 5:26 we see that Christ has chosen us to be His bride.

I am sure that the celebration at Joseph and Asenath's wedding was an awesome festival with music, dancing and rejoicing, but the wedding feast of Christ and His Church, which is yet to come, will far surpass anything that this world has seen, can afford or even imagine.

Praise and Promotion

Pharaoh said in Genesis 41:39-41, *"'...Inasmuch as God has shown you all this, there is no one as discerning and wise as you. You shall be over my house, and all my people shall be ruled according to your word; only in regard to the throne will I be greater than you.' And Pharaoh said to Joseph, 'See, I have set you over all the land of Egypt.'"*

In comparison Jesus said in John 15:16, *"You did not choose Me, but I chose you and appointed you that you should go and bear fruit, and that your fruit should remain, that whatever you ask the Father in My name He may give you."*

The Lord has ordained our lives to bring change to the people around us. The wisdom we receive through the Word of God and His Holy Spirit is meant to become our spiritual authority, drawing our world to the kingdom of God.

The following Scriptures are reminders to us of Joseph's promotion linked to our position in Christ. Ephesians 1:18-23:

> *"The eyes of your understanding being enlightened; that you may know what is the hope of His calling, what are the riches of the glory of His inheritance in the saints, and what is the exceeding greatness of His power toward us who believe, according to the working of His mighty power which He worked in Christ when He raised Him from the dead and seated Him at His right hand in the heavenly places, far above all principality and power and might and dominion, and every name that is named, not only in this age but also in that which is to come: And He put all things under His feet, and gave Him to be the head over all things to the church, which is His body, the fullness of Him who fills all in all."*

Ephesians 2:6:

> *"and raised us up together, and made us sit together in the heavenly places in Christ Jesus, that in the ages to come He might show the exceeding riches of His grace in His kindness toward us in Christ Jesus."*

Paul elaborates on our risen Lord's exalted position, and threads in our position of being raised up and seated in heavenly places with Christ. John further bears this out in Revelation 3:21:

> *"To him who overcomes I will grant to sit with Me on My throne, as I also overcame and sat down with My Father on His throne."*

Due Respect

Genesis 41:43: *"and they cried out before him, 'Bow the knee!'"*

The homage and honor given to Joseph is symbolic, once again, of that which the church must willingly exhibit at the Name of Jesus. Philippians 2:10-11 declares, *"that at the name of Jesus every knee should bow, of those in heaven, and of those on earth, and of those under the earth, and that every tongue should confess that Jesus Christ is Lord, to the glory of God the Father."*

The definition for "knee" in Strong's # 1120 is, "to bend the knee or knees to someone;" it also means "to kneel in homage and adoration."

"Every knee" that we have must bow to the authority, glory, and purpose of Jesus Christ. We need to let our goals, yearnings, ambitions, inspirations, advancements, and motives be 'knees' that bow to God's will.

Christ commands us to love Him with all that we have. This is just another way of saying that all our ambitions must be motivated by our love for God.

Pharaoh said that nobody should go anywhere or do anything without Joseph's approval. Colossians 3:17 states a close parallel to Pharaoh's command. *"And whatever you do in word or deed, do all in the name of the Lord Jesus, giving thanks to God the Father through Him."*

THE SEVEN YEARS OF PLENTY

The wedding is over, and Joseph is into his first week at the palace. We stand aside and marvel as we see him address many of the king's servants as if he already knew their names, position and status in Egypt's parliament. What do you think...was he functioning through divine revelation?

Our answer is, "no!"

Joseph has been serving most of them in the king's prison for the past years. Joseph knows their tales of deceit, he remembers those who were rude, rebels and undependable. He also knows those who are worthy of promotion. As a youth, he had been trained to listen to his brothers' tales so he could bring the report back to his father. Now this training has paid off.

This is one reason the king can entrust Joseph with the responsibility to:

Be lord over his house.

Be ruler over all his possessions.

Bind his princes at his pleasure.

Teach his elders and senators wisdom. (See Psalm 105:21, 22)

Joseph already knows who can be trusted with responsibilities of building granaries or of supervising the planting of crops. He knows who he can work with because he knows the character and strengths of the people to which he is assigned.

The sureness of the dreams' interpretations are so real in both Pharaoh's and Joseph's hearts that they have little trouble convincing the nation of the coming famine. As Joseph travels back and forth and up and down in the land, the king's subjects have no doubt concerning the truth of the dreams' interpretations. They respond readily to Joseph's detailed instruction of how to harvest, what to keep for their own needs, and where to store the rest.

Joseph readily paraphrases Proverbs 31:21 for anyone who complains of the hard work or long hours. "We won't be afraid of the famine because we are laying up crops against those unproductive years" he answers.

Joseph, an optimist, holds keys to make the land productive. The Bible teaches us that it brought forth by abundance and was more fruitful than it had ever been before. Joseph is also a teacher of preservation. He appreciates what he has and values the crops in light of the disaster that lurks on the horizon.

Clearly, Joseph knows how to live in financial freedom and prosperity. Even though he knows the famine is just a few short years down the road, he isn't consumed with a doomsday mentality. Instead he taps into every available resource to fortify the land against the time of drought.

It is during the first seven years that Asenath bears Manasseh and then Ephraim. Manasseh means 'one who forgets,' while Ephraim means 'double fruit.' Joseph realizes that God is calling him to forget the details of the past, so that he can be doubly fruitful. His sons' names remind him of God's favor and plan. Later, both sons will be named in Joseph's place among the twelve tribes of Israel.

In our lives we also must give birth first to Manasseh, one who forgets, before we can experience the double fruit of Ephraim.

HOW WOULD WE RESPOND TO A FORTHCOMING FAMINE?

Listen in as Joseph gives the long term weather forecast for Egypt: "Ladies and gentlemen, the king has just had two dreams that foretell our long-range weather. There will be seven years of great plenty here in Egypt. There will be great abundance, but don't be fooled. After this affluence there will be seven years of horrible famine in all of the land."

How will you respond to today's forecast? Will you pack your bags and head across the border or remain right where you are? Will you be productive during the time allotted you, or will you make excuses about the paganism surrounding you or your heathen mate?

I'm not telling anyone what to do about having a family, but the point here is that we need to be full of faith as Joseph was! No matter what famines await us, lack of faith is not an acceptable excuse for not being productive in the various aspects of our lives. Joseph wasn't fearful of raising children who would be exposed to famine and spiritual filth alike!

Each time Joseph said the names of his sons, he reviewed God's goodness. Joseph wasn't in a dither, wondering if he could raise his sons to be God-servers.

As we see God using Pharaoh, an evil king of a pagan land, to place Joseph into the position of becoming a savior to his father's house, so God wants us to realize that He can use our most desperate situations to bring us to the place of fulfilling our destiny.

Hopeless circumstances are not meant to separate us from God's love or His plan for us.

WHAT YOU HAVE LEARNED

It doesn't take God even a day to rearrange your situations.

God summons each of us into His presence.

The gifts Pharaoh gave Joseph are comparable to the gifts Christ gave the church.

The fine linen garment emphasizes our Godly character.

The king's ring symbolizes our spiritual authority.

The gold chain represents us being set apart to the Lord.

The new name is the reward for the overcomer.

Joseph's bride parallels the church, Christ's bride.

Promotion seats us in heavenly places in Christ Jesus.

The master deserves our respect.

AN EXERCISE TO PRACTICE

Read Ephesians 1:18-23 and Ephesians 2:6, 7 in your favorite version of the Bible and write out your own paraphrase of these two portions of Scripture.

_____

_____

_____

CHAPTER ELEVEN

Joseph's Dreams Fulfilled

~ *Genesis 44-47* ~

L ook at the heaps of grain and the barns full of corn! There had been seven years of abundance unlike any Egypt had ever seen before. Seven years of calling all manpower to action for sowing, planting and cultivating. After that had come the harvesting, thrashing, storing and preservation of both food and water. There is plenty of all that the land can produce.

During these seven years, Joseph has stayed focused on the task at hand though we wouldn't have faulted him if he'd tried to get a message of his promotion to his father. We wouldn't criticize Joseph if he'd made a nighttime escape for Canaan as his father had done when he left Laban. He could have readily excused the action as needing to alert his family of the upcoming famine, but Joseph made no such moves or excuses.

Because of Joseph's respect for his position and because of his diligent work, the granaries are filled to the roofs and spring has arrived. Farmers wait for the usual rains, but all they get is merciless sunshine. People carry buckets of water just to grow a few fresh vegetables and keep their cattle alive.

Joseph faithfully stays on top of who is buying what from where. He proves completely trustworthy as he travels throughout the land to see to the welfare of his subjects. His faith in God surpasses the severity of the famine and grounds his integrity.

THE FAMINE REACHES CANAAN

Well into the second year of famine ten men appear on the eastern horizon. After Joseph's twenty-two years of testing he still recognizes his brothers, though they don't recognize him. He speaks only through an interpreter to them and makes himself stern in their presence.

"Who are you?" he demands of them.

Terrified, they answer, "We are ten brothers and we have come to buy corn in Egypt."

Joseph accuses them of being spies and further inquiries about their families.

"We are all the sons of one man, and we have another little brother at home who is unable to leave his father," they falter.

"Why do you say he's unable to leave his father?" Joseph flings back at them.

The brothers squirm uncomfortably as they look to each other for a spokesman. Finally, Reuben clears his throat and says, "Our father had twelve sons, but one is dead, and the little one is his full brother. Our father fears that something dreadful will also happen to the youngest one."

Joseph presses them hard for answers concerning his father. "The old man, he is still alive then?"

"Yes," the answer comes back, "our father is still living."

Joseph remembers his brothers' cruelty and decides to test them to see if they've changed.

"You're spies and just making up a lie about having a little brother," Joseph accuses them. He commands that they all be bound and imprisoned for three days.

Afterwards Joseph releases them and says, "I've changed my mind because I fear God. Instead of sending just one of you to bring back your little brother, I will send you all back to Canaan except for one. The rest of you may take food to your families, but you won't be permitted to buy more food in Egypt unless you bring your youngest brother with you. Is that understood?"

To Joseph they nod as if they had understood, but they immediately began to argue and blame each other for this horrible moment. They know full well that they have brought this weighty instant onto themselves. But who wants to take the blame for coming into wrong agreements with each other? They had woven a horrible web of soul-ties by never confessing their deception and sins to their father. Because of their evil deeds, the doors for attack from their oppressor are standing wide open. They are at fault and they all know it!

Reuben, trying to justify himself, reminds them that he'd tried to rescue Joseph, but they hadn't paid any attention to him. Blaming, after twenty-two years of unconfessed sins, has no power to free any of the brothers from their guilt. The brothers have no idea that this ruler can understand them and knows what they are arguing over, but Joseph remains silent, watching and listening.

Joseph eyes the terrified brothers as he chooses the one who is deemed to be the cruelest among them to be kept as a prisoner. Try to imagine the alarm Simeon feels as he is chosen, bound before his brothers, and put into the prison where Joseph himself had served.

The servants, following Joseph's command, have filled the brothers' sacks with corn and restored their money into each sack.

Wiping sweat from their brows the brothers hardly dare to breathe as they set out toward home—leaving Simeon behind. Turmoil overwhelms them when they get to the inn for the first night and each finds his money restored in his sack.

They finally come to the place of bringing God into the picture. One asks, "Do you think God is trying to teach us something through this?"

Conviction pricks their hearts, but none of the brothers are willing to confess what they'd done. Even the imprisonment of Simeon has not penetrated their calloused hearts. And yet the dilemma still remains…how will they explain this horrible turn of events to their father? Will they finally be forced to tell the truth about Joseph after all these years of living and hiding a horrible lie?

BACK IN CANAAN

When they return to their father, pride wins out and they suppress the truth further. They speak only of the governor's unreasonable demands.

Fear grips Jacob's heart when he hears Benjamin is to be taken into Egypt. The door to rage is flung wide open. "Why did you tell the governor that you had a little brother?" he demands.

They try to explain that the governor was very intimidating and direct with his questions. "He seemed to ask just the exact questions that forced us to disclose more than we were comfortable with. What else could we do besides giving him an answer?"

All too soon the corn from Egypt is gone, and Jacob commands the brothers to return for more. When the brothers hear Jacob's demand, they all come together to make an appeal to their father. They feel as if their lives are at stake.

"Father, we know that we will starve without food from Egypt, but we cannot go without our little brother. We have to bring Benjamin with us!

Jacob's heart is set against Benjamin going along, but the brothers argue, "Look, there are only nine of us here! Simeon is back in the horrible dungeon we told you about. Do you want the rest of us to wind up there too? Do you love Benjamin more than you do all the rest of us put together?"

Even though this hits a sensitive note in Jacob he remains unrelenting.

Reuben, seeing his father's distress, finally humbles himself, "Father, send Benjamin with me, and if I fail to bring him home you can kill my two sons."

Still Jacob remains unmoved, refusing to send his son!

The brothers choose death by starvation over death by Egypt's ruler which they assume will be their fate if they return without their brother.

Desperation and famine force Jacob to call his sons one more time. He commands these grown men to go and buy food in Egypt. The same argument ensues until Judah finally breaks before his father. With tears rolling down his cheeks he pleads, "Father, we would be back with food for the second time if you'd only sent Benjamin with us. Send our brother with us and I will assume full responsibility for your son. I'll bear the blame the rest of my life if I don't bring him back to you."

Jacob has convinced himself that the worst is about to happen. He expresses this in Genesis 42:36: *"You have bereaved me: Joseph is no more, Simeon is no more, and you want to take Benjamin. All these things are against me."* when he finally relents, releasing Benjamin to accompany his brothers his parting words express his resignation. "If I am bereaved of my children, I guess that's just how it has to be."

TO EVERYTHING THERE IS A TIME

Joseph had been placed in the position where he would eventually see his dreams fulfilled, and yet he has to wait. Joseph has seen his brothers – one of them is still within arm's reach in his prison house!

Daily his eyes search the horizon for the return of his brothers, but they have not come. He realizes that their corn must have been consumed by now. How easy it would be to release Simeon and send him home with more corn for those he loved.

He, no doubt, dreams of sending for his father, his nieces, and his nephews to bring them into Egypt to be close to him. It would be effortless to jump in to bring relief to all of them. But he understands and realizes the exact moment of revelation must be in God's set time. This period of waiting is a time in which he searches his own soul for right attitudes and is a time for praying for his family.

Joseph's frequent looks toward the eastern horizon challenge him with questions, "Will his father send his younger brother with the others? How long will it be?"

A STRANGE TURN OF EVENTS

When the brothers return to Egypt they are sent to the house of the stern governor. They are terrified and conclude it is because of the money that had been restored in their bags. Judah steps forward to make an appeal to the servant in charge of them. He offers to repay the money they had found in their bags.

The servant assures the brothers that he had received their money.

Judah hovers close to Benjamin to be sure that no harm will come to him as they are led into the great hall of the Egyptian ruler. The stately pillars that had greeted Joseph nine years earlier now greet the brothers. They are hard put not to have their presence announced by their footsteps echoing through the grand corridors of Joseph's home. Benjamin clings to Judah as he stares at the shimmering marble floors and unbelievable expanses of the vaulted ceiling.

"We've never eaten in such a lavish place before," the brothers whisper to each other.

They anxiously await the governor's fury but instead they are treated with respect and warm hospitality. Simeon is brought to them and looks none the worse for his prison time.

The brothers greet him in whispered tones and ask if he knows what is going on. Simeon hasn't a clue! The brothers can't believe their eyes! The table is lavishly set, and they are seated in the order of their age. Joseph's plate is missing, and the brothers still assume him dead. Joseph sits alone as food is served to his brothers. A portion five times as big as the other's is served to Benjamin, who seems to be the center of attention.

It is difficult for Joseph to eat, for he longs to embrace his full-blooded brother! Because of his longing he escapes to his chamber to weep. He wants them to know that he has forgiven and loves them. He yearns to reveal himself to them, but he knows further humility is needed.

As Joseph returns Dan is boasting, "Wait till we tell Father about this feast and the luck we have in eating with the governor." He is completely unaware that Joseph understands them all.

They are gloating as they leave Joseph's house with their sacks filled with corn, and unbeknown to them, their money and Joseph's divining cup in Benjamin's sack. They had come with trepidation but have been given the honor of eating with the governor himself! Simeon is elated to be back with the clan, Judah is breathing lighter because he has Benjamin by his side and each prides himself in escaping without revealing his past sins.

Suddenly their merriment turns into dead silence! Someone is calling to them. They immediately stop and look back. The servant who had helped them saddle their donkeys is now approaching them angrily.

"How is it that you repay good with evil?" he demands of the eleven.

"The governor put himself out to make a great banquet for you, but you have had the audacity to steal his divining cup right out of his house! How dare you think that you can escape without punishment for such a crime!" the servant cries out.

The brothers feel that their father's prediction concerning Benjamin's disappearance is about to come true! Judah is about to lose his freedom! The brothers' consciences are screaming the words from Numbers 32:23, *"Be sure your sins will find you out!"*

Guilt, blame, unconfessed sins, and cruelty all swirl about them, making this moment seem surreal.

"We didn't steal from the governor, your honor," the brothers plead. "Remember how we brought our money back that we found in our sacks from the other time, so why would we steal from you now?"

The search begins and the cup is found in Benjamin's sack…a planned intervention to bring the brothers to complete humility and repentance! Joseph's strategy works and the brothers return in humility and trepidation.

Judah, true to his promise, steps forward to protest the imprisonment of his young brother. He offers that they will all be prisoners, but that Benjamin must be released.

The governor, however, discounts the plea and says that Benjamin is guilty and must remain his prisoner.

Judah tells Joseph the whole episode with their father, emphasizing that if Benjamin does not return their father will die of grief.

I AM YOUR BROTHER

When Joseph sees the repentance, the humility, and the tears of his brothers he cannot restrain himself any further. He realizes that this is the moment he has been waiting for to see his dreams fulfilled!

Joseph calls for everyone to leave the room except for the brothers. The air is charged with extreme and mixed emotions as Joseph speaks in the Hebrew tongue for the first time. "I am your brother, Joseph. I am the one that you sold into Egypt!"

Immediately terror strikes the hearts of the brothers! Suddenly they realize their vulnerability! The ten older brothers tremble and cower from the presence of Joseph, knowing he has the authority to imprison them. Benjamin stands in total bewilderment. How could this be? He has been told over and over that a man-eating beast had devoured the brother he loved in his childhood, but now this man says he is his full-blooded brother! How could this strange Egyptian be related to him?

Judah, having assumed the responsibility for his youngest brother, now has to confess that they had sold his full-blooded brother into Egypt. What a moment of revelation!

Now each man has to deal with his own sins, his own lies and his own cover-ups. Their deceitful lifestyle has erupted in their faces, and the lies they have lived can no longer continue! Confession will have to be made to Jacob because Joseph is sending wagons into Canaan to bring him and the whole clan into Egypt.

In the end God's truth has prevailed! Joseph's patience, faith and pursuit have paid off! The promises God has given are fulfilled! The long awaited moment has arrived! The longing of Joseph's heart has come into total agreement with God's Word, and he has received the full reward of God's destiny for him!

In this moment the brothers, who we would likely consider unfit to be forgiven, receive the full embrace of their savior, Joseph! They can do nothing but accept Joseph's grace in humility, knowing they have done nothing to earn what he is doing for them.

Joseph realizes that his brothers have a long journey to come to the place that God wants for them. His heart is full of compassion and not revenge. He doesn't boast an 'I told you so' attitude. He has mercy and not retaliation and tells them, "God has sent me before you to prepare a place for you and your families. You meant this for evil to me, but God meant it for good to all of us. We are only in the second year of a seven-year famine. I am supplying you with wagons and supplies so you can bring my father and your families into Egypt, where I will take care of you." Then as an afterthought he says, "See that there's no arguing along the way!"

THE BROTHER'S CONFESSION

Joseph has retained his brother, Benjamin, but the others are on their way. Joseph's supply and wagons are following them. The brothers have a difficult time with conversation. "This is 'the dreamer,' and his dreams have saved us," Judah ventures.

Reality hits home. They will have to humble themselves to their father and confess their lifestyle of lying. It was not only the initial lie they told, but the whole web of lies.

Jacob has been anxious and has awaited his son's return. Will they have Benjamin with them? Their delay in returning has further escalated Jacob's fearful thoughts. By the time the brothers have returned he immediately searches for his youngest son. Benjamin is missing!

Jacob cries out in anguish, but the brothers who have decided to share the blame quickly explain that their brother is well and that Joseph is still alive. Jacob doesn't believe them until they confess their guilt and how that God has actually used their injustice to bring their own deliverance in time of famine.

At the announcement, Jacob is on the verge of having a heart attack! The brothers point out the carts Joseph has sent and show him all the provisions for Jacob's journey into Egypt.

It doesn't take Jacob long to load his family and head into Egypt where he meets the son that he was sure had been dead for many years!

What a moment that must have been! The dreams that Joseph had clung to through some of the most difficult times in any person's life are now a reality! On the other hand, Jacob's lies that he had clung onto throughout his years of testing were proven to be just that…lies! The son who had lived by the faith in God's Word sees the reality of the things he had lived for! The father, who could have clung to the visitations God had given him, has lived a life of disappointment and pain. In this moment of reunion his unbelief is banished!

At their first meeting Joseph falls on his father's neck and weeps a good while, but Jacob's faint-hearted thoughts are still death-centered. He says in Genesis 46:30, *"Now let me die, since I have seen your face, because you are still alive."* Jacob has lost his vision for a future with the son who had shared his dreams with him. He had failed to realize that the God who gives dreams will also fulfill them. He has no dreams of sharing the last years of his life with the one he mourned for so many years, but just asks to die.

Joseph, however, nourishes his father and gives him possession of the best of the land.

LET'S EVALUATE JACOB'S CONCLUSION

When Jacob had seen Joseph's torn and blood-dipped coat twenty-two years earlier, he had spoken a self-curse onto himself. He refused comfort, saying his head would go down to the grave in sorrow. The lying evidence of Joseph's coat became a monument of pain that he chose to revolve his life around. Every time he recounted the pain, he built a stronger resistance to God's grace.

Jacob stated four flat-out lies in Genesis 42:36. The evidences justified them, but God's promises didn't. Nevertheless, he actually believed that Joseph and Simeon were dead, that he would be robbed of Benjamin, and that all these elements were working against him.

We have seen earlier how God had visited Jacob, and now he had to come up with more and more excuses of why he wouldn't allow God to resolve his issues. He had come into agreement with deceitful facts that annihilated the truths God had given him during his days of visitation.

The difference between father and son here is that Joseph dealt with his self-curses, his strongholds, his soul-ties and the generational curses that he had inherited, while Jacob had wasted a big portion of his lifetime believing lies. He had hung onto all his soul-junk and refused the fire Joseph embraced for his cleansing and liberation. The cleansing fire Jacob refused to embrace became a festering wound and blocked God's peace from his soul.

In comparison, the fear in Jacob's heart and the faith in Joseph's heart work through the same components of their mind, will and emotions. The only difference is that Jacob hangs onto defying facts while Joseph holds fast to God's promised truth. The attitude each chooses makes all the difference in their individual outcome.

These comparisons between father and son—of faith and fear, when remembered, will help us walk in faith when circumstances rise up, as dark monsters, to dominate our thought patterns.

We must avail ourselves of God's ever-present grace and plan ahead to hold onto God's promises no matter what! We can simply state that we won't agree with lying evidences, the enemies' lies or our own soul-junk. If God spoke the word, we can trust it!

Each promise that He has given us has criteria of faith for us to meet and a timetable in God's sovereignty to fulfill.

THE ULTIMATE IS YET TO COME

Jesus, the bridegroom who has waited long centuries for his bride, has been revealed to us for His saving and keeping grace, but the time for His debut as the appointed heir of all things is still awaiting Him! (Hebrews 1:1, 2) Patiently and eagerly He waits to display His glorious church!

When our Savior condescended to be clothed with humanity, being stripped bare of his Heavenly vestures, he took upon Himself the form of a servant and became obedient to death. Because of this, God also raised His Son up from the dead and has given Him a seat at His own right hand on His majestic throne in Heaven. Although this whole series of events is beyond our human understanding and can only be embraced by faith, we must believe the best is yet to come! The fullness of time has not yet arrived for Christ to unveil His magnificent bride, His church! Christ's final vision is yet to be fulfilled!

The vision Jesus has of His resplendent church can be seen in Revelation 21:9-11.

> *"Then one of the seven angels...talked with me, saying, 'Come, I will show you the bride, the Lamb's wife.' And he carried me away in the Spirit to a great and high mountain, and showed me the great city, the holy Jerusalem, descending out of heaven from God, having*

the glory of God. Her light was like a most precious stone, like a jasper stone, clear as crystal."

This holy Jerusalem represents us, the saints of God, the overcomers, who have entered by faith into His kingdom.

Even Isaiah the prophet had an insight into what God will reveal in the last day—that great day that Christ is still waiting for. Look at Isaiah 62:1, 5: *"For Zion's sake I will not hold My peace, And for Jerusalem's sake I will not rest, Until her righteousness goes forth as brightness, And her salvation as a lamp that burns. For as a young man marries a virgin, So shall your sons marry you; And as the bridegroom rejoices over the bride, So shall your God rejoice over you."*

We are part of the bride that is adorning herself with Godly virtues in preparation for that great eternal marriage. This life on earth becomes our expedition of preparing for this wedding feast.

In II Corinthians 11:2, Paul says that he has wooed the Corinthians so that he might present them as a chaste virgin to Christ.

As a mother who has had the privilege of helping three daughters prepare for their weddings, I have a minute understanding of Christ's excitement as He awaits this longed-for marriage. Revelation 19:7-9 exhorts, *"...Let us be glad and rejoice and give Him glory, for the marriage of the Lamb has come, and His wife has made herself ready." And to her it was granted to be arrayed in fine linen, clean and bright, for the fine linen is the righteous acts of the saints. Then he said to me, "Write: 'Blessed are those who are called to the marriage supper of the Lamb!'"*

Christ Jesus still awaits the appointed time to reveal His fullness, and to embrace His bride when we step into His eternal kingdom! We saw the emotions that Joseph displayed as he revealed himself to his brothers, but what do you think that Christ's debut will be like? I am sure that it will be beyond all prior imagination and glory!

This is why I say, "the best is yet to come!" Christ has still to reveal His Church. She will be gloriously arrayed, and more so than Joseph was in his fine linen garment; for she will be clothed with all the virtues of Godliness.

WHAT YOU HAVE LEARNED

Joseph's dreams actually were fulfilled after twenty-two years of testing.

Joseph had to be patient for the exact moment in God's timing.

Joseph attributed credit to God and did not blame his brothers for the things that had befallen him.

Jacob's and Joseph's choices were based on the same components of the soul, but they had different results because of their perspectives.

We have tools available through Christ within us, which enable us to live a victorious life.

Christ is still waiting for His dream to be fulfilled, when He will take us, His Church, to be His eternal bride.

AN EXERCISE TO PRACTICE

The concepts of this book demand change within each of us. It is helpful for us to avail ourselves to effective ways of praying. The following prayer example will lead you into God's presence and help you embrace His refining work in your life.

Almighty and everlasting God, Creator of heaven and earth, I come to you in the Name of Jesus, who has redeemed me through His shed blood on Calvary.

I come to give You honor, for You are worthy of praise. You are worthy to be exalted in all I do and at all times. I choose to crown you the Lord over my mornings when I awaken. I choose to declare Your praises at noontime and when darkness falls.

Though I wait long for Your promises to be fulfilled, I worship you through my long hours and tears. Your truth remains the same. You are unchanging in Your divine nature as seen in Your creation.

I loosen myself from any distractions of Your grace. I call every thought that disagrees with Your decree for me a sin. I repent of these sins and avail myself of Your forgiveness and cleansing. I appropriate Christ's blood on Calvary to give me the lifestyle of an overcomer.

I call for every emotion that is just hanging around to come and kneel at Your cross and declare Your Lordship! I require everything in my past to proclaim Your love for me. I decree that each event of my future shall align itself with the empowerment of the resurrected Lord and that my life will be filled completely with Your Holy Spirit. My choice is to focus on You and Your Word that I may know that You will cause the outcome to be according to Your plan.

Thank you for Your love, Your wisdom, Your faithfulness and Your anointing in me.

In Jesus' name, Amen.

Jacob in the Joseph Generation

~ Genesis 47 and 48 ~

*B*efore the third year of famine is over, Joseph has settled his father and brother's families into the land of Goshen. Goshen is a 900 square-mile area around the Nile delta and because of irrigation is considered to be some of Egypt's best land. Joseph nourished his 130 year old father and the 70 people who came with him out of Canaan with the best possible provision that the famine could offer.

Pharaoh had appointed this property for Joseph's family and had also sought out some of his brothers to become occupied in the care of his own cattle. The famine had been hard, but all of Jacob's family was well cared for. Jacob finally allowed himself to indulge in the blessing of seeing God's salvation in time of famine. He had time to reflect on Joseph as a youth. He remembered the dreams God had given him and with that he started recalling his own past and how God had intervened on his behalf.

JACOB'S BIRTH AND BOYHOOD

We have journeyed with Joseph for over 40 years of his life, but we have basically seen only the outgrowth of Jacob's life. We have seen him as a man who had believed lies concerning things that were difficult for him to bear. We have seen him come into wrong agreements with bitter circumstances and give in to fear rather than rising up in faith.

There are, however, areas of Jacob's life that we have not taken into consideration and we must do so in order for us to understand the blessing that he will pass on to the generations after him. In Hebrews 11:21, 22 Jacob is listed in God's '*Hall of Fame*'. Regardless of what happened in the early part of Jacob's life, God was still at work in and through him.

As we see life unfold in this great forerunner of our faith we must consider ourselves lest we also be tempted. (Galatians 6:1b)

Rebekah, Jacob's mother, may be considered to have been a 'mail-ordered' bride. Abraham, Jacob's grandfather had sent his oldest servant, Eliezer, back to Mesopotamia, to find a bride for his son Isaac. This beautiful love story unfolds in Genesis chapter 24. Eliezer was divinely guided by God to Abraham's brother, Nahor's family. There Eliezer met Rebekah at the community well and was given permission by her family to bring her back as a bride for Isaac. Rebekah, the adventuresome and eager one, came willingly to a strange land to be married to her second cousin.

Isaac married Rebekah after Sarah, his mother, died. He brought her into his mother's tent and made her the first lady of their land. He loved her and found comfort in having her in his life.

Even though Isaac loved his new bride and was considerate and caring of her in her strange new surroundings, she was unhappy because for 20 years she was unable to give birth to a child.

Isaac went before God and entreated Him, praying fervently on behalf of his barren wife.

The God who had spared his life on Mt. Moriah when he was a 13-year-old now gave heed to Isaac's heart-felt prayer and opened Rebekah's womb. She found herself pregnant with the first twins recorded in Scripture.

Jacob's birth is an interesting account recorded in Genesis 25:19-26. Rebekah's pregnancy was unusual in that her sons were struggling within her womb. Rebekah, perplexed by the matter, found a place where she could seek God and asked Him concerning her condition.

"Since you answered my husband's prayer for a child, why is all this turmoil going on inside of me? I feel as if I can hardly breathe and the constant commotion keeps me from sleeping at night." As Rebekah made her supplication to the Lord, He answered her.

"You will not have identical twins because there are two different kinds of people inside of you. These will be leaders of two diverse nations. The one nation will be stronger than the other and in the end the oldest brother will serve the younger one."

When Rebekah's time of delivery was at hand she gave birth to two sons. The first one came out hairy and red, but the second one came out smooth. Not to be outdone, he grasped his older brother's heel. The twins who had struggled in their prenatal confinement continued to struggle with each other as they grew into young men.

Esau became a hunter and roamed the fields, giving little attention to spiritual attributes or values. Isaac loved Esau the firstborn of the twins because he ate the venison which he prepared for him. His adventuresome disposition plunged him into a heedless lifestyle and opened the doors for him to be deceived by his younger brother, Jacob, known as the supplanter. He found himself checkmated by his brother and defrauded of the best things that life could have given him.

He was to receive the blessing of the birthright which would afford him both spiritual and material blessings. Because he didn't value this heavenly gift, he bargained it away for a bowl of Jacob's pottage. He had arrived home from a day of hunting in the fields with nothing and declared that he was famished to point of starvation.

Jacob was his mother's favorite, perhaps because she had received the promise that he would be the leader. As it plays out she stepped in to play 'god' in this situation. These young men were called to be a prince with God, but each led their own selfish lives. Rebekah didn't help the situation any. She instigated the scheming to have Jacob receive the blessing that Isaac was preparing for Esau. Rebekah had instructed Jacob to lie and deceive his father. (Genesis 27:1-33)

Because Jacob had purchased the birthright from his twin brother for one bowl of red bean soup, and then had sneaked off with his blessing, Esau was furious with him. Too late, Esau had awakened to the fact that he had lost God's best to his little brother and he was out to get revenge. He wasn't quiet about his feelings and Rebekah heard that he planned to kill his brother as soon as their father died.

JACOB IN PADAN-ARAM

By this time Isaac was an old man and his eye-sight was nearly gone. In this account we can plainly see the soul-ties between Rebekah and her son, Jacob. He was being guided by his mother who was trying to force God into doing things her own way.

Ishmael was Isaac's half-brother, the son of his mother's slave. God had promised Abraham that Ishmael would become great, but that Isaac was the promised son onto which the birthright and blessing was to be passed.

Esau, knowing that the people of the land were not those chosen by God, married into the tribe of the Ishmaelites. Rebekah went to Isaac and told him that she was tired of her life since Esau had done this thing. She insisted that Jacob should be sent back to her homeland and find his wife from among her relatives.

Isaac called for Jacob and spoke a prophetic and poetic blessing over him before sending him back to Padanaram to the house of Rebekah's family.

Isaac's beautiful language revealed his spiritual perception as he sent his son away to find a wife. Even though he was to find a wife in Haran, he was to be mostly concerned with entering into the spiritual inheritance of his forefathers. He was to call on El Shaddai as his God. Through the father's blessings Jacob received a challenge, a command and the promise of fruitfulness, multiplication and the assurance for his journey.

JACOB LEAVES HOME

The parting of ways was not as it should have been. There was division in a marriage that started out so beautifully. The parents had each played favorites and doted on the son of their choice.

Isaac had not stepped up to the plate to pass the blessing on to the son that God has specifically chosen. Rebekah had tried to force things to happen, Esau was angry and revengeful and Jacob was heading into life alone—leaving behind him his mother whom he would never see again.

Even though Jacob left home in an unfavorable way, God was with him. The first night as the sun was setting he gathered stones for his pillow in a certain place. I can well imagine that he may have felt alone out in the open that night. However, he did fall asleep and dreamed of a long ladder that was set up on earth and had a top that reached into heaven.

As the dream progressed there were angels that ascended and descended upon the ladder. As Jacob looked up into heaven he saw the Lord standing at the very top of the ladder looking down on him.

The Lord introduced himself saying, *"I am the LORD God of Abraham your father and the God of Isaac; the land on which you lie I will give to you and your descendants. Your descendants shall be as the dust of the earth; you shall spread abroad to the west and the east, to the north and the south; and in you and in your seed all the families of the earth shall be blessed. Behold, I am with you and will keep you wherever you go, and will bring you back to this land; for I will not leave you until I have done what I have spoken to you."* (Genesis 28:13-15)

As Jacob awoke he realized that the angels of God had started ascending the ladder right from the very spot on which he was lying. This would indicate that God's angels had been at the exact place he was sleeping. The dream also proved that they were still there. God's angels had not only ascended but also descended.

Jacob thinking he had been alone said out of fear, "Surely the Lord was right here in this place and I didn't even know it! This place is awesome and it can be called nothing but the house of God and the gateway into heaven!"

Before leaving that place Jacob set up the stone he had used as a pillow and turned it into a pillar. He poured anointing oil on it naming it Bethel, meaning the 'House of God.' He made a vow to God at that sacred spot.

"...If God will be with me, and keep me in this way that I am going, and give me bread to eat and clothing to put on, so that I come back to my father's house in peace, then the LORD shall be my God. And this stone which I have set as a pillar shall be God's house, and of all that You give me I will surely give a tenth to You." (Genesis 28:20-22)

JACOB AT LABAN'S HOUSE

Jacob's journey continued until he came to his uncle (his mother's brother) Laban's house. The community well was a common gathering place and this well could easily have been the same spot where Eliezer had met Rebekah. Rachel, Jacob's first cousin came with Laban's flocks and Jacob rolled the stone from the well's mouth and watered her sheep.

It was after this that he kissed Rachel and revealed to her who he was. Jacob lifted up his voice and wept and Rachel ran to tell her father that his nephew was at the well,. It had been years since Laban's sister had ridden off on a camel with Eliezer, and he was elated to receive her son—his nephew into his home.

As time progressed, Laban hired Jacob to care for his sheep. When he asked Jacob what his wages should be the young man readily replied, "If you will give me your beautiful daughter, Rachel, to be my wife I will serve you for seven years."

Jacob deeply loved Rachel and it seemed but a short time for him to serve the seven years. However, the injustice that he had deceived his father and his brother with was coming back to him. On his wedding night he was deceived into marrying Leah, the older and less attractive sister. Laban required Jacob to give her a week of festivity and celebration before he could marry his second daughter, Rachel. The stipulation with this was that he would serve another seven years for her after that.

Now Jacob found himself in the predicament of have to work another seven years and having a second wife which he didn't love. The sisters became enemies and fought over who would get to sleep with their mutual husband.

They had another problem and that was that they were both barren. Barrenness was considered to be a piteous situation in those days. The competition continued as did their prayers. The Lord listened to Leah's petitions and opened her womb. She bore Jacob six sons and a daughter. Each time she hoped that her husband's heart would be tuned to her for the gifts she bore him.

Rachel's hurt cut deeply as it was mixed with envy and jealousy towards her sister. The competition ran a bazaar course until Rachel gave her handmaiden to Jacob to bear her sons. When Leah realized that she was no longer bearing children she followed suit. Through this revengeful means, four more sons were added to Jacob's family.

Rachel never gave up the fight and finally the Lord gave her the desires of her heart. Joseph was born! You have already read his story so we will continue in order to see how all this plays out in the life of Jacob.

Jacob served Laban for another six years during which time Laban changed his wages ten times. God was with Jacob and continued to give him wisdom to increase regardless of the change in wages. Laban and his sons became envious of God's blessings in Jacob's life until God sent His angel to Jacob and instructed him to return to his father's house.

JACOB MEETS ESAU

Lord had sent an angel to Jacob and instructed him to return to his father. His wives agreed and they fled by night for fear of Laban. The earlier practices of injustice in Jacob's life were having a boomerang effect. He headed back to his father's land with fear and trepidation. Esau was still alive and Jacob had no way of knowing if he was still plotting to murder him.

When Jacob heard that Esau was coming to meet him with 400 men, fear mounted in his heart. He prayed to God and flung himself completely on His mercy. He then prepared lavish gifts of livestock and sent them before him. After that he sent his most valiant men to the forefront of what may become a battle. He divided his family by clans and kept Rachel and Joseph in the rear—closest to him. Then he sent them all ahead of him and he remained alone in the night.

During the night a man came to him and Jacob contended for a blessing without receiving it. A wrestling match ensued until the angel put Jacob's hip out of joint. Finally, as day was breaking, the angel insisted on leaving but Jacob was determined that he would not leave without receiving that blessing.

The angel told him that he contended as a prince of God. Then he asked Jacob his name, and he answered, "Jacob". The angel continued, "You will no longer be the supplanter, Jacob, but you are now given a new name. Your name is Israel which means 'he who prevailed as a prince with God'.

The angel left and Israel's contrition and perseverance during a night of sleeplessness had paid off. He had received the promise he needed to meet the challenge of the new day.

Because that Israel's hip was out of joint, he hobbled into the dawn of that day. A breakthrough had come and the two brothers met in peace. Esau accepted Israel's generous gifts though he protested at first. Israel sent Esau ahead of him as he led his clan on more slowly for the sake of the children and young cattle.

Sadly, Rachel died on that journey while giving birth to Benjamin, her second son. This struck great sorrow in Israel's heart, but it also released him to love the mother of Judah who would perpetuate the Messianic line.

ISRAEL BLESSED HIS OFFSPRING

And now Israel was relocated in Egypt, and his family with him. Age was creeping in and he was coming to the end of life's journey. Even though he had experienced many sorrows, had been misled and had come into wrong agreements with others, he moved beyond these obstacles and bore God's promised blessings. God had spoken and He was still able to perform His promised blessings.

Somewhere during his time in Egypt, Joseph brought his sons to meet their grandfather, Israel. The old patriarch seems almost overwhelmed to get to meet these fine young men when he had never dreamed of even seeing Joseph again.

He said that these two boys should be considered to be his own sons as if he was adopting them. He also said that they were to be brought under the covenant of God's people and were to be tribal leaders. In this way Joseph was given a double portion of God's blessings.

Israel had been blessed by his father and he knew the need to pass the blessing on to the future generations. He also had divine revelation concerning his grandsons. When Joseph brought them in to meet their grandfather he had a special blessing for them. Manasseh was the oldest so Joseph automatically thought he would receive the greatest blessing. Because of this he guided Manasseh toward Israel's right hand and Ephraim toward his left.

The aged prophet wittingly crisscrossed his hands, placing his left hand on the oldest son and the right on the youngest. When Joseph saw what was happening he tried to return his father's hands to the son's head which he considered to be the right one.

Israel assured all of them that he knew what he was doing, that as in his own case, the older son would be subject to the younger one.

At the end of Israel's life we see him arise and sit on the side of his bed to fulfill the purpose for which he was called. In Genesis 49 he calls his sons to tell them what would befall them in the last days, and to address each of them with words of blessing, reprimand—or curse. Israel's summon begins with his oldest son, Reuben and ends with Benjamin his youngest.

Rightly he pronounces the blessing on Judah to be the perpetuation for the royal Messianic line. He praises Joseph for being fruitful even when he was hated and shot at by archers. Each son received a word of admonition, exhortation, encouragement or a curse from their father.

These last moments in the life of Israel was what he lived for. If he had made wiser choices earlier in life these moments may have come sooner or the story may have had a slightly different slant, but none of it would have changed God's power to bless.

Israel, after finishing the blessing, gave final instructions concerning his burial and pulled his feet into the bed on which he sat. There, without any expression of remorse, unforgiveness or fear he breathed his last breath.

ISRAEL DID NOT HINDER GOD

As we have basically fast forwarded through the last 25 chapters in Genesis, we have touched a few of the highlights in the life of Israel. We have seen enough of his self-inflicted pain that we know things could have been different for him, but in his case we see that experience was his best teacher.

Something else that we see here is that God literally fulfilled Romans 8:28 in the life of Israel. *"For we know that all things work together for good to those who love God, to those who are the called according to His purpose."*

There is no question in the life of Israel as to whether he was called of God as we have watched Abraham pass the blessing to the future generations. He had arisen to impart the same to his sons and grandsons.

There is also no question concerning his love for God. Genesis 34:1-4 tells us that God visited Israel and told him to return to Bethel to build an altar of worship. This was the place where God had met him at the top of the ladder that had reached from earth to heaven. He immediately called his family and commanded them to bring all the gods that they had collected from the nations around them. They were also to bring him the earrings which they were wearing in order to cleanse and ready themselves to appear before God. Israel hid all the strange gods and earrings under an oak tree in Shechem, thus showing his love and devotion to the God of his calling.

One of the two points that I want to make at the end of this chapter is that God is not hindered from fulfilling His plan just because we goof up. I am not advocating that we go out and put ourselves in harms way of sin. I am not endorsing the concept that we can sin and then just expect God to forgive us.

God told Noah that His Spirit will not always strive with men. (Genesis 6:3) Thus He had Noah build an ark to rescue his family from the coming flood that destroyed every living thing that was outside the ark.

When we give in to sin after we are born again, we are giving sin dominion over us. Romans 6:14 plainly tell us that sin has lost its power to dominate us when we come to know Christ. God is calling us to the righteousness, peace and joy of His kingdom. With this in our hearts, we can be sure that God is able to fulfill His complete work in and through us.

"For with God nothing is ever impossible and no word from God shall be without power or impossible of fulfillment." (Luke 1:37 AB) This verse means that God can do anything and everything, but putting it another way we can say, "Nothing is impossible with God." We see that "nothing" is not in God's daily routine. "Nothing" is not something God practices.

From this we can see that God can do "all things," but he will never be found "doing nothing." This should bring us comfort and assurance. When we allow ourselves to become detoured from God, He is still at work on our behalf. We need to quickly turn around and go back to Him. God will not deny our contrite and repentant heart.

God is able to do above and beyond all that we can ask in prayer, desire in our hearts or hope in our dreams. (Ephesians 3:20) Israel's life surely bears this out.

WE MUST RAISE UP A JOSEPH GENERATION

Most of *Beyond the Colorful Coat* has been about our own relationship with Christ. It has been a study that leads us to our own spiritual development and maturity. But this chapter has to do with passing the blessing on to future generations. Israel's basic call in life was to raise up sons that would become the blood-line through which Christ, our Messiah, would come.

He had many confirmations that he was to pass the blessing on to those coming after him, and this is exactly what we are called to do. We have learned many things from the examples of Joseph's life and now **it is imperative that we pass them on** to those who are succeeding us.

In the day which we are living we must raise up young and spiritual warriors. These warriors can only be truly victorious if the older generation will pass the baton successfully to the younger one. I have heard the saying that every young warrior needs an old war horse. In many cases this is not happening today. Here are some of the reasons for the gaps the older generation is leaving between them and the younger.

Pleasure seekers—living the American dream.

Sickness, doctor visits, pharmaceutical medication—living life in a drugged state.

Lack of vision—feeling there is nothing left for them to do.

Laziness in the lifestyle—very little study of God's Word and prayer.

Fear of our youth—the fear of not being understood and then rejected, or even the fear of being assaulted by them.

The sense that they had finished their work—quitting before the blessing was passed down on them.

Many other reasons—simple distractions that come from not specifically setting focus and goals.

On the other hand, our youth are also leaving vast gaps in their communication which make for a lack of unity.

Disrespect for parents—this is a Scriptural requirement.

Lost in the world of technology—something that the older generation doesn't readily understand.

Peer pressure—the claim that everyone is doing it.

Not learning from discipline—reacting rebelliously to correction.

No love for God—having no due respect or reverential fear of God.

Ungodly counselors and teachers—not being established in the absolute truth of God's Word.

I am of the older generation and because of the tests and trials I have experienced, I also know the healing love and infinite grace of God in many areas of my life. I have learned things about making personal application of God's Word for various and difficult situations.

I am not alone in this boat. There are many senior citizens who could share a testimony of how God has brought them through the storms in their lives and has blessed them. These have wisdom to impart to young families or teenagers.

I cry when I think of the youth of our day who are receiving their input from many various sources—sources that divert them from hearing seasoned ministers who share God's Word. They lack the encouragement that they need as they plunder into life on their own terms.

We must uphold this generation so that they can be men and women who will be trained, encouraged and enlightened by God's truth which will never change. The best way this can happen is for parents and grandparents to become involved in their children's lives.

Some of this parent-generation could become a spiritual partner rather than a physical parent. I challenge my generation to become involved with our younger people. Now is the time that we must come alongside parents who are struggling with balancing budgets, bouncing babies and building strong relationships. We must take the hand of our teens and slow their pace a bit and teach them wisdom. If we do not do this, they will learn through much hardship—we will be passing them a curse instead of a blessing.

If you are of the younger generation and are reading this book, you have a great tool to train yourself with—ask someone from the older generation to mentor you.

If you are in the older generation and have this book I, encourage you to find a younger person with which to walk this spiritual walk.

Here are a few points to cling to and/or to pass on from the examples of Joseph's life:

God loved Joseph—we must love the generation coming after us, or the one who has come before us.

Joseph kept himself morally pure—each generation must require this of the other.

Joseph prevailed beyond only having dreams—he saw them fulfilled.

Joseph kept his life free from bitterness—he embraced his difficulties.

Joseph remembered God's promises—the blessings that enabled him to move beyond his problems.

Because of all these virtues, you as a younger person have a prize which is yours to reach out and grasp. We as the older generation have the same prize to pass on. No matter which generation we find ourselves in we have a responsibility to our family, our church, our community and our nation. Let us pass on Israel's blessing—the proclamation of the Gospel of Jesus Christ!

WHAT YOU HAVE LEARNED

Jacob is moved from being a supplanter to being Israel—a prince with God.

Israel loved God and was chosen by God.

God was not hindered from fulfilling his promises because of Jacob's faltering faith-walk.

God anointed Israel to pass on the blessing.

The older generation is responsible to impart God's blessings onto the younger generation.

The younger generation must be responsive to receive correction, instruction and impartation from godly leaders.

AN EXERCISE TO PRACTICE

An exercise for the older generation:

Copy the following Scripture verse and write out who you will take under your wings and how you will serve them.

> *"And the things that you have heard from me among many witnesses, commit these to faithful men who will be able to teach others also." II Timothy 2:2*

_____

_____

_____

_____

_____

_____

_____

_____

_____

An exercise for the younger generation:

Copy out the following Scripture verse and write down the name of the godly mentor that God wants for you. Then go to that person and ask them to spend time in your life and impart their God-given wisdom to you.

"Let no one despise your youth, but be an example to the believers in word, in conduct, in love, in spirit, in faith in purity. Till I come, give attention to reading, to exhortation, to doctrine." I Timothy 4:12, 13

_____

_____

_____

_____

_____

_____

_____

_____

_____

The Coat of Mourning

~ Genesis 50:1-6 ~

*A*s we step into this final scene, our hearts will break. A great man has died and Joseph feels the sting of it more than the others. God had given him back his father for the past seventeen years. Now the father he has nurtured is gone! We will note that Joseph retains his integrity and maintains God's presence as he passes through this time of mourning.

We watch as Joseph dons his coat of sackcloth along with the other mourners. As he clothes himself with the same garment the others are wearing he puts himself into the same rank as the rest of his family and all those in Egypt who are mourning with them. For a time, he has lost his identification as the prince over the land of Egypt. Nevertheless he is still fervent in his spirit toward God.

He remembers his early years back in Haran when his father had told him stories of faith and how God has blessed him with a time of healthy bonding during Jacob's twilight years.

Genesis 49:22-26 records these words:

"Joseph is a fruitful bough,
a fruitful bough by a well;
his branches run over the wall.
The archers have bitterly grieved him,
shot at him and hated him.
But his bow remained in strength,
and the arms of his hands were made strong.
By the hands of the Mighty God of Jacob
(from there is the Shepherd, the Stone of Israel),
by the God of your father who will help you,
and by the Almighty who will bless you
with blessings of heaven above,
blessings of the deep that lies beneath,
blessings of the breasts and of the womb.
The blessings of your father
have excelled the blessings of my ancestors,
up to the utmost bound of the everlasting hills.
They shall be on the head of Joseph,
and on the crown of the head of him who was separate from
his brothers."

In essence Jacob tells Joseph he has learned Godliness from his grief, obtained healing in his hurt, and triumphed over his trials. These words upheld him and empowered him to continue maintaining the presence of God.

OUR WORK IS NOT YET FINISHED

As the times of storm move into our lives the need for us to develop more Christian attributes will always be a reality.

For us to discontinue developing Godly characteristics in our lives would be like rowing our boat upstream, finally spotting our destination on shore, and putting down our oars. Before our spiritual nap would be over we'd find ourselves back where we started. We must never stop rowing our spiritual boats until we are anchored by eternity in the life hereafter.

With a heavy heart the second highest authority in the country, clothed in his coat of mourning, joins the Egyptian forty-day embalming ceremony. The seventy-day mourning for his father involves much weeping, self-abuse, and throwing of dust. Joseph mourns with his brothers and the Egyptians until it is finally time to bury his father.[1]

Because of Jacob's request to be buried in Canaan, Joseph's task is not complete at the end of the seventy days of mourning. He still has to receive leave from Pharaoh to bury his father. (Matthew Henry's Commentary, footnote 2 under Ch. 50) states, "He observed a decorum, in employing some of the royal family, or some of the officers of the household, to intercede for this license, either because it was not proper for him in the days of his mourning to come into the presence-chamber, or because he would not presume too much upon his own interest."

Joseph knows that it is not an acceptable custom for anyone to come in before the king with the attire that symbolizes sorrow. It doesn't matter that Joseph has already been governor over the land of Egypt for twenty-six years.

The whole process of his father's death and mourning has been a humbling experience for Joseph, as he had to put off his royal robe and put on one of lowly position. Because of his need, he requests his servants to intercede for him to the king.

We see this marvelous heart of humility in Joseph. We may seldom realize how much humility it took for Joseph, a high official in Pharaoh's house, to bow to the same level as Pharaoh's slaves. This humility gave Joseph the ability to start at the bottom of his pain and work his way up to complete healing. For this season he had to die to his former dreams of being the lord over his brothers and the whole country of Egypt.

JESUS THE ULTIMATE EXAMPLE OF HUMILITY

Jesus is our greatest example of humility. He and Joseph draw many parallels in scripture, and both their examples of humility are amazing.

Paul paints a word picture of Christ's humility in Philippians 2:5-8. *"Let this mind be in you which was also in Christ Jesus, who, being in the form of God, did not consider it robbery to be equal with God, but made Himself of no reputation, taking the form of a bondservant, and coming in the likeness of men. And being found in appearance as a man, He humbled Himself and became obedient to the point of death, even the death of the cross."*

Christ's own humility brought Him from Heaven to earth. The Son of God rode a donkey, wept, hungered, and slept. He dealt with the emotions of compassion, love and mercy. Even though He is the Son of the Almighty, and even though he could have delivered Himself from any sort of death, He humbled Himself to go through the sufferings of humanity by dying on the cross.

Talk about 'power under control'…that was and is Jesus! He thought modestly of His own importance so He could become all we needed for our spirit, soul and body. The apostle Paul lived with this consciousness, and that is why he urges us to let the mind of Christ be in us. In essence he is saying, "Be humble as Christ was. Don't try to dodge the table of suffering that Christ partook of."

Humility lays a solid foundation for life, whereas pride never does. Pride builds with self-centeredness which enthrones oneself and ultimately ends in defeat, but humility serves the lowliest and ultimately is ushered to the top. Though humility is not a popular concept in today's society, it was a characteristic that helped Joseph maintain God's presence in his life.

Humility cannot be humiliated for it is dead to pride. Humility will never suffer from being humiliated because it has already dealt with the heart issues that would resurrect self. Steps of humility that are viewed by many as steps leading downward, actually lead upward.

Can you see the progression of humility being formed in Joseph's life? First he served in prison, then in the king's courts, and finally his own family?

Jacob's beloved son bows before his servants and asks for their help during his time of dilemma. His humility grants him the king's permission to bury his father some 300 miles away.

THE BROTHERS' REQUEST

Upon the family's return from the burial of their father, the brothers' conscience bothers them once more. They remember the wrong they had inflicted on Joseph who is now in a position to avenge himself of their evil deeds. As they speculate that Joseph could change his mind concerning them, fear grips their heart.

The brothers timidly approach Joseph with their appeal, "Before our father died, he told us to tell you not to avenge yourself on us for our past sins."

Joseph's answer is one of humility. "It is not in my heart to get revenge for what you have done. You had thought to harm me and treat me cruelly, but God knew He would employ me in Egypt to bring salvation to His people. God is the one who sent me here, so don't blame yourselves about the past. Now is the time to move ahead with the tasks at hand."

What graciousness! He is completely releasing his brothers from the guilt of their past and freeing them to come back to Egypt with him. His answer released them from the old mindset that had kept them enslaved.

Humility allows Joseph the freedom to be human without crushing his dignity, self-worth and purpose. His humility keeps him pliable in the hands of God and gives him the power to be great.

JOSEPH DISPLAYS ACCOUNTABILITY

We don't see Joseph retiring at the usual age of sixty or seventy, but he continues to maintain his kingly virtues up to his death at the age of 110. What a testimony! What an example!

One of the things that have made this long-reigning governor so outstanding is the fact that he was always accountable. He was never guilty of fraud, embezzling funds or using a paper shredder to destroy documents. Joseph was never dishonest or neglectful.

Joseph was accountable in his moral standards. He never had an affair with his secretary. He didn't take his bookkeeper to lunch without having a companion with him. He abstained from all appearance of evil. As a youth he paid the price for moral purity and he never allowed himself to be sucked into that vice later when he was at the top of the ladder. He was a one-woman man, and God honored him for that.

A great preacher once excused his immorality by making the excuse that he was on top of the ladder with nobody over him to be accountable to. This preacher's supposed position was man-made and not God-made. God does not put us into precarious places and then step away to watch us fail.

James understood this. James 1:13, 14 says, *"Let no one say when he is tempted, 'I am tempted by God': for God cannot be tempted by evil, nor does He Himself tempt anyone. But each one is tempted when his is drawn away by his own desires and enticed."*

There were never any headlines in Egypt's newspapers stating, "Governor of Egypt has an Affair," or "Joseph, Egypt's Governor, is Guilty of Fraud."

The one good thing we see from his childhood is that he had learned about accountability when he reported his brother's whereabouts as a youth. We see his accountability to the prison keeper in his prison experience. This great prince was accountable to the God of his ancestors and the faith they had taught him. We have no reason to believe that Joseph was ever untrue in any way. Having established this character before becoming a ruler, he knew the importance of having advisors and mentors.

James 5:16 commands us to confess our faults, trespasses errors, mistakes, and wrongdoings to one another and then to pray for each other.

I believe that Joseph surrounded himself with men of worth who stayed faithful to him. He chose men of integrity, senators that he himself had trained, to hold him responsible for his words and actions. He understood Proverbs 11:14: *"Where there is no counsel, the people fall; But in the multitude of counselors there is safety."*

Throughout the life of Joseph his plans fall into place, and the whole nation of Egypt flourishes because he sought counsel. His plans are established and the concept of Proverbs 15:22 is plainly evident in his thought-patterns.

In I Corinthians 4:2 the apostle Paul commands, *"Moreover it is required in stewards that one be found faithful."* Then in verse 4 he makes an interesting statement when he says, *"For I know of nothing against myself, yet I am not justified by this; but He who judges me is the Lord."*

Anyone who will be accountable and go the FAR road with God must maintain these three ingredients as a lifestyle.

>**F**aithfulness
>**A**ccountability
>**R**elationships

Accountability is the strong link sandwiched between faithfulness and relationship. God, our final judge, will require this of us. In the previous chapter you read about the need for having these relationships, now you see the need for these in a 3-D perception. I urge you to establish relationships on earth with those who will dare ask heart-searching questions of you. Then be accountable to God by spending time in His presence.

GRACE: THE ULTIMATE INGREDIENT

There are two different kinds of grace. The first is the saving grace of our Lord Jesus Christ that we appropriated into our lives in the very first chapter. This is the grace we experience as we take Jesus to be our Savior and our Lord. But there is also grace given to us to live by.

Humility and accountability are two elements of our own soul that we must maintain to remain in God's plan; these cannot substitute for the grace of God to live by.

Grace is a gift we cannot buy, for grace becomes the "it" in Jesus' dying statement on the cross when He cried out, *"It is finished!"* His provision of grace on our behalf was finished. Grace is available to us in each of our situations. Grace is the currency of the kingdom of God. By it we can acquire all that we need to move us beyond ease and into a victorious spiritual walk.

Grace closes the gaps that our humanity leaves. It bridges the point where our ability stops to where God's divinity begins. It fulfills God's requirements which we cannot fulfill by our own determination. Grace perfects the things that concern us and fulfills all His other promises to us.

God doesn't want us to veer, reel or steer away from our tests in life, but He wants to bring us through them. Hurt and pain are meant to initiate tears of healing. These are to be embraced.

Sheer willpower brings hardness of heart. The refusal to confess our needs is also the refusal of God's grace and leads to legalism.

Self has no power to fulfill what grace fulfills in a person's life which is governed by faith and love.

Grace can be depended on, built on and clung to without leaving us dangling by the bare string of our emotions.

I believe that the only reason that you've read to this point in this book is because the Lord has drawn you. God's saving grace and His to-live-victoriously grace are the reasons for this book. If we were to go back and reread this book solely to see God's grace at work in Joseph's life, here are a few things we'd see:

It was grace that caused Joseph to remember the God of his great-grandfather on his journey into Egypt.

It was grace that helped him sort through his soulish conflicts to the point where he even became the prominent slave.

It was grace that kept him from immorality when Mrs. Potiphar's nudity and seductiveness pressured him.

It was grace that gave him the heart to serve in the prison.

It was grace that gave him wisdom to interpret the king's dreams.

It was grace that gave him a forgiving heart toward his brothers.

It was grace that allowed him to have seventeen years with his father.

It was grace that allowed him to live to the age of 110.

SOME THINGS GRACE CAN DO FOR US

Grace shines us God's light in our darkness.

Grace maintains the presence of God in desperate surroundings.

Grace calls sin "sin".

Grace prevails over defeat.

Grace triumphs over our felt weakness.

Grace stimulates the believer to exercise faith.

Grace proclaims the same things God does.

Grace awakens us to the truth of God's written Word.

Grace is available to us through faith in Christ Jesus and the love of God.

Grace is a mountain-moving part of God's timetable.

Grace is the Christian's ammunition against his enemy.

The list of what grace is, what it does, and where it comes from could go on endlessly, but that is not the important factor here. The thing of importance is that we understand that as God's grace was with all of His children, so that same grace is still available to each of us in every stage of life.

WRITE YOUR OWN CONCLUSION

To help you remember some of the concepts you learned throughout this book, go back and write an outstanding point for each of the ten chapters.

Chapter 1

_____

_____

_____

Chapter 2

_____

_____

_____

Chapter 3

_____

_____

_____

Chapter 4

_____

_____

_____

Chapter 5

_____

_____

_____

Chapter 6

_____

_____

Chapter 7

_____

_____

Chapter 8

_____

_____

Chapter 9

_____

_____

Chapter 10

_____

_____

Chapter 11

_____

_____

_____

Chapter 12

_____

_____

_____

Chapter 13

_____

_____

_____

Summary

_____

_____

_____

_____

_____

_____

_____

_____

_____

_____

_____

_____

Joseph the Foreshadowing

of Jesus

Joseph:	**Reference to Jesus:**
Was loved by his father	Matthew 3:17
Left his father to find his brothers	Phil.2
Was rejected by his brothers	Is 53:3
Was thrown into a pit	Is. 53:4; Luke 23
Was sent to a certain death to fulfill God's will	Heb. 5:9
Was appointed heir to his father	Heb. 1:2
Was a shepherd	John 10:14
Exposed his brother's sins	John 1:4
Was rejected by his own	John 1:12
Was envied and hated	John 15:18
Envisioned a coming kingdom	Matthew 24
Was almost killed by his brothers	Matthew 26

Was stripped of his royal robe	Matthew. 27
Was sold for silver	Matthew 27
Wept over his brothers	Matthew 23:37
Fellowshipped with his brothers	I John. 1:7
Was sent ahead	John 3:17
Told his brothers to go back and tell…	Mark 16:7
Was given a bride who would give him sons	Is. 62:5
Suffered injustice	Is. 53:6
Had no bitterness toward men	Luke 23:34
Was totally yielded to God	Luke 23:46
Was completely helpless without God	Matthew 27:46
Was ready to be a leader	John 10:10
Wholly accepted his circumstances	Matthew 26:64
Was aware of his need to depend on God	John 17
Was a prisoner	Matthew 26:57
Was a hated Hebrew	John 8:59
Was elevated to second in command	Eph. 1:20

Endnotes

Chapter One: The Robe of Righteousness

1. Merrill C. Tenney, *Zondervan's Pictorial Bible Dictionary,* Zondervan, Grand Rapids, Michigan 49530, 1967, p.227
2. Ibid., p. 226
3. Ibid., p. 226

Chapter Two: Robe of Many Colors

1. Spiros Zodhiates, Th.D., *The Complete Word Study Dictionary of the New Testament,* AMG Publishers, Chattanooga, TN 37422, U.S.A., 1992, p. 66, #26
2. Merrill C. Tenney, *Zondervan's Pictorial Bible Dictionary,* Zondervan, Grand Rapids, Michigan 49530, 1967, p. 345
3. Ibid., p. 226

Chapter Three: Dothan and the Refining Process

1. L. Thomas Holdcroft, *The Pentateuch,* Western Book Company, Oakland, California 94612, 1966, p. 42

Chapter Five: The Journey

1. James Strong, S.T.D., L.L.D., *Strong's Exhaustive Concordance,* Baker Book House, Grand Rapids, Michigan, Old Testament Ref. #6884

Chapter Seven: The Slave's Garment

1. James Strong, S.T.D., L.L.D., *Strong's Exhaustive Concordance,* Baker Book House, Grand Rapids, Michigan, Old Testament Ref. #2114
2. W. E. Vine, M.A., *Vine's Expository Dictionary of New Testament Words,* MacDonald Publishing Company, McLean, Virginia 22101, p. 37; 210

Chapter Eight: The Prison Garb

1. Ron A. Bishop The Joseph Story, Treachery, Betrayal and Redemption Palm Tree Publications P.O. Box 122 Keller, TX 76244 www.palmtreeproductions.net , p. 58

Chapter Ten: The Royal Robe of Authority

1. Merrill C. Tenney, *Zondervan's Pictorial Bible Dictionary,* Zondervan, Grand Rapids, Michigan 49530, 1967, p. 724
2. Ibid., p. 151
3. Ibid., p. 907
4. Ibid., p. 75
5. Ibid., p. 609

Chapter Thirteen: The Coat of Mourning

1. Finis Jennings Dake, *Dake's Annotated Reference Bible,* Dake Bible Sales, Inc., Lawrenceville, Georgia 30246, 1963, p. 50
2.

Reference on Joseph

BC1729	Joseph with his father, Jacob in Canaan	Gen 37:1-2
	Age 17 Coat of many colors	Gen 37:1-2
	Joseph dreamed dreams	Ge 37:5-11
	Joseph sold	Ge 37:27
BC 1729	Joseph in Potiphar's house	Ge 39:1-19
	Joseph in prison	Ge 39:20-23
BC 1720	Joseph, butler's and the baker's dreams	Ge 40
	Joseph still forgotten	Ge 40: 23
BC 1715	Pharaoh dreamed dreams	Ge 41:1-32
	Joseph speaks a word of wisdom	Ge 41:33-36
	Joseph promoted to ruler over Egypt	Ge 41:37-45
	13 years of testing	Ge 41:46
BC 1707	The brothers come for provisions	Ge 42
	Joseph revealed himself to his brothers	Ge 45:3
BC 1706	Jacob comes to Egypt	Ge 46

Writing
A Book?

Should you be writing your own book? Before you start, call us. Our company's best selling point is our honest, live-person assistance. We're here to guide, critique and share the joy

LIFE SENTENCE
Publishing, LLC

715.223.3013
www.lifesentencepublishing.com